MARCO ⊕ POLO
PRAGUE

KU-268-888

with Local Tips
*The author's special recommendations are
highlighted in yellow throughout this guide*

*There are five symbols to help you find
your way around this guide:*

for Marco Polo recommendations - the best in each category

for all the sites with a great view

for places frequented by the locals

where young people get together

(A1)
map references

(0)
outside area covered by map

MARCO ⊕ POLO

Other travel guides and language guides in this series:

Algarve • Amsterdam • Brittany • California • Crete • Cyprus •
Florida • Gran Canaria • New York • Paris • Mallorca
Rhodes • Rome • Tenerife • Turkish Coast

French • German • Italian • Spanish

*Marco Polo would be very interested to hear your
comments and suggestions. Please write to:*

*World Leisure Marketing Ltd
Marco Polo Guides
9 Downing Road, West Meadows
Derby DE21 6HA England*

*Our authors have done their research very carefully, but should any errors or
omissions have occurred, the publisher cannot be held responsible for any injury,
damage or inconvenience suffered due to incorrect information in this guide.*

*Cover photograph: Old Town and Charles Bridge (Bilderberg/Madej)
Photographs: Janfot (12, 15, 29, 31, 62, 70, 78)/Kallabis (32, 44, 53, 55, 60, 69, 87, 91,
inside front jacket); Mauritius: Enzinger (82); Hubatka (4, 18); MacLaren (47, 76, 81);
Rawi (48); Torino (8, 64); Witzgall (38)*

Cartography: Mairs Geographischer Verlag, Hallwag

*1st English edition 1997
© Mairs Geographischer Verlag, Ostfildern Germany
Author: Lubor Vorel
Translation: Andrew Bredenkamp
English edition: Cathy Muscat, Emma Kay
Editorial director: Ferdinand Ranft
Design and layout: Thienhaus/Wippermann
Printed in Italy*

CONTENTS

Discover Prague 5
The royal and imperial city enters a new golden age

Exploring the city 13
Castles and kings, Gothic splendour, princely palaces...
all the riches of a magical city brought back to life

Cultural riches 39
The extensive Prague art collections include bohemian
Gothic, Dürer's 'Rosenkrantzfest', the diamond
monstrance, nineteen Picassos and other Cubist works

Eat your heart out 49
Prague's Vinarna have been serving excellent wine and
culinary specialities for centuries

A shopper's paradise 65
On the Golden Cross, you can buy Bohemian glass
and dark-red garnets, chic fashions, antiques and
traditional crafts

A good night's sleep 71
Luxury hotels and converted palaces, bed and breakfast
or a room in a private house - there is something to
suit every pocket, but be sure to book in advance

Prague diary 79
There is no shortage of top class entertainment,
from classical concerts to tennis tournaments

Out on the town 83
Opera and ballet, classical concerts and jazz, cabarets
and clubs, brass bands and Romany songs...
entertainment for every mood

Practical information 89
Important addresses and other useful information
for your visit to Prague

Do's and don'ts! 94
Some tips on how to avoid the traps and pitfalls
the unwary traveller may fall into

Index 95

What do you get for your money 96

Discover Prague

*The royal and imperial city enters
a new golden age*

There are few countries in the world that boast a city as beautiful as Prague. In this respect I would venture to say that the capital of Bohemia by far surpasses such great cities as Nuremberg, Vienna, Wroclaw or Cologne. I would even go so far as to suggest that neither Rome, Venice nor even Florence can compete with the beauty of this pearl in the heart of Europe.'

Perhaps King Rudolf's nuncio was exaggerating a little in his declaration, but it is nevertheless an indisputable fact that Prague is one of the most beautiful cities in the world. As London is associated with Big Ben and Buckingham Palace, Paris with the Eiffel Tower and the Seine, the classic image of Prague that springs to mind is that of the royal castle of Hradčany, a magnificent Austro-Hungarian structure that rises majestically above the Vltava river as it flows serenely through the Gothic arches of the Charles Bridge.

View of Prague Castle, the Little Quarter and the Charles Bridge

Alongside Athens, Rome, Paris and London, Prague is one of the most historic cities in the West. No other city has as many epithets attached to it: the Golden City; the City of a Hundred Towers; the Symphony of Stone, Colour and Shape; the City of Legends; the City of the Golem, of Kafka, of Schwejk…

The kings and emperors of Bohemia summoned the best architects in Europe to their court to build magnificent holy and secular buildings. In an area of just 800 hectares there are somewhere in the region of 2000 buildings of architectural and historical importance. These include around 70 noble palaces, 80 churches and 35 monasteries. Appropriated 40 years ago by the communist regime, all religious buildings, including the famous Strahov Monastery, have now been restored to the Catholic Church.

Prague has been occupied by many different races in its long history, most notably the Czechs, the Germans and the Jews. This cohabitation, though sometimes discordant, gave rise to some spectacular cultural and economic results. The Second World War, however, divested Prague of its rich cultural diversity when the virtual extinction of the Jews was followed by the expulsion of the Germans. The Czechs had little time to recover from the horrors of war and rebuild their community. One tragic period was followed by another, much longer, era of darkness as the 'iron curtain' descended. From the East came a new dictatorship, which lasted some 40 years, during which Stalinism exercised unrelenting control over the lives of the Czech people. In the 1950s a monument was erected to honour the tyrant. It was such a monstrous construction that the sculptor committed suicide after it was unveiled. For several years after Stalin's death, the memorial dominated the Letná hill on top of which it stood. To the relief of the people, it was eventually blown up in the 1960s. This was a symbolic act — as Brecht said 'The great do not remain great'.

Then in November 1989 students, artists and ordinary citizens awoke to a new dawn. Like Sleeping Beauty after the prince's kiss, the dormant beauty of Prague began to wake. The city rubbed the sleep from its eyes and slowly restored itself to its former splendour. Although many of the great houses and palaces had suffered damage over the years (and money for restoration was seriously lacking), the new government decided to open all the important monuments which had been closed to the public for so long. The delightful Royal Gardens complete with its great Renaissance ball-game court, the gardens of Prague Castle, Vrtba garden, the terraced gardens at the castle ramp, the beautiful Gothic Charles Hall in the Old Royal Palace, the residence of the Bohemian kings and princes: all were made accessible. Even the famous Triforium gallery in St Vitus Cathedral with its 21 remarkably life-like busts (1374-85) is now open for all to admire. Just recently the Knight's Hall in the Wallenstein palace (the first Baroque palace in Prague) was opened for concerts. Named after its architect Valdštejn (Wallenstein), who built it in the 17th century, it became the headquarters of the Ministry of Culture, which, during the totalitarian regime, was dubbed the 'Anticulture Ministry'. The current ministry is housed in the colossal Černín Palace. In 1948 the then Foreign Minister Jan Masaryk was found dead beneath one of these windows, shortly after the communist putsch. Officially it was reported as suicide, but all the evidence pointed to a 'fall from a third floor window' — one of the many so-called 'defenestrations' to occur in the city's history.

Although it will be a long time before the country recovers fully from the economic, ecological and moral problems caused by the communist regime, the people of Prague have already begun to shed their sad and resigned expressions, and western tourists are no longer struck by that morose and afflicted air that once characterized them.

So what is the true character of the people of Prague? In the 1960s the Prague-born German writer Johannes Urzidil wrote: 'The Czechs were considered for

Walking through Prague

Imperial Prague

For the best views of the Royal Castle, the Charles Bridge, the Little Quarter and St Nicholas church, follow the riverside walk between the National Theatre (**E4**) along Smetanovo nábřeží as far as the Čechův bridge (**E2**). This walk is even more magical at night when the whole area is beautifully lit.

Art Nouveau in Prague

Explore the lovely Art Nouveau area around Pařížská street (**F2**), across Staroměstské náměstí and along Celetná (**F3**) to the finest example of this architectural style, the municipal house, Obecní Dům, on Náměstí Republiky (no 5). No 7, Na příkopě, the beautiful Art Nouveau Hotel Evropa with its splendid interior at no 29, Wenceslas Square and Peterka House at no 12 are worth a closer look. Other notable Art Nouveau buildings are at 13 Ulice 28. října, 34 Jungmannova, 16 Masarykovo nábřeží and 7 and 9 Národní třída.

Historical Prague

Stroll through the narrow lanes of the Old Town around the Powder Tower. This is the start of the Coronation Procession, which runs across Staroměstské náměstí, along Karlova, over the Charles Bridge and up the steep Nerudova to St Vitus Cathedral where, for centuries, Bohemian kings were crowned (**F3-D2**).

House signs

Introduced in the 14th century to facilitate orientation of the city, there are around 2000 of these historic signs left dotted around the city. The best of them can be seen around the streets of Celetná (**F3**), Karlova (**E3**) and Nerudova (**C-D 3**). Don't miss the sign of 'the three fiddles' at number 12 Nerudova, a house owned by three generations of violinists from 1667-1748.

In Mozart's footsteps

Mozart loved Prague.
'The people here understand me' he said, after his disappointing receptions in Vienna and Salzburg. He lived with the Dušek family at Uhelný trh 1 (**F3**) (marked with a plaque) and in the 'Bertramka' (**C5**) where the Mozart museum is now housed. He played for guests in the salon of Count Pachta z Rájova on Anenské náměstí, and the Estates Theatre (**F3**) held the premiere of 'Don Giovanni'.

Picturesque Prague

Malá Strana (the Little Quarter) is an enchanting part of town in which to lose yourself. Apart from the Baroque splendour of the countless aristocratic palaces, the historic wine bars provide good food and drink. The best point of departure is the metro Malostranská (**E2**)

long periods of time as a warlike and aggressive people, lively and full of initiative, particularly when they were able to rely on natural or elected leaders; but we have also seen long intervals of passive, sad resignation, interspersed with flashes of uprising and rebellion. This duality is plainly visible in the music, art and literature of the Czech people.' In the light of this assertion, Václav Havel is perhaps the ideal leader of the newly emerging Czech republic.

The peaceful 'Velvet Revolution' of November 1989 brought a significant change to people's lives. The inhabitants of Prague often refer to events as occurring 'before or after the November'. It has become a landmark in time. Before November 1989 political jokes were commonplace; now you will rarely hear any. The irony previously used as a defence mechanism against the hardship of everyday life under the communist regime is no longer necessary. Likewise *Schwejkism,* aimed at attacking the stupidity of violent authority, is no longer relevant in this new democracy. The negative cynicism which was once a characteristic trait of the people of Prague has been replaced with positive commitment, energy and initiative. This explains the sudden emergence of hundreds of private workshops, shops and travel agents all over the city. Prague has been given a new lease of life.

Prague now attracts more tourists than Venice or Florence. On the one hand this invasion annoys the inhabitants; they love their city and the river that runs through it and often get angry about the polluted air and congestion that fills their streets. On the other hand they are proud and happy that the world is interested in their city and eager to see its treasures.

Although restaurants' prices have shot up because of the influx of tourists, the locals still like to eat out regularly... when they can find a table not occupied by foreign visitors. At weekends, however, they load up their cars and

The Wenceslas Monument on the long Václavské náměstí

> **Prague Cobbles**
>
> Many of the pavements in Prague are decorated with mosaics of coloured marble, and the roads are mostly cobbled. The cobblestones, however, have greatly deteriorated over the last 40 years as they were not properly maintained. A drive through the bumpy town is referred to sardonically by the locals as the 'Prague Rally'.

drive off to their *Chata* (weekend house) or *Chalupa* (old farmhouse), happy to escape the city for a couple of days. This is why at weekends you will probably only come across fellow tourists in Prague, hanging out in the U Fleků with its 30% proof beer, in the U Tomáš with its black beer or in the U kalicha with its 12% Pilsner. Most of the visitors around these central watering holes are German, while the Italians flock to the bars of the Little Quarter (Malá Strana) to savour the wines from South Moravia. The most popular international rendezvous has for some time been the picturesque Zlatá ulička (Golden Lane) which is almost too narrow to cope with all the visitors.

With all the buskers, singers and hawkers, the magnificent Charles Bridge is not wide enough to accommodate the flocks of people from all over the world who have come to admire the Baroque statues that decorate this wonderful open-air museum. Legend has it that wine and egg shells donated by all the Bohemian parishes were added to the mortar when the bridge was built to strengthen it — perhaps the only reason it does not collapse under the weight of so much human traffic. There may actually be some truth in this,

since recent studies have revealed that the mortar does in fact contain organic material. Six hundred years on, the locals still joke that the wily citizens of Velvary brought their eggs hard-boiled.

Pride and interest in their history is a characteristic of the people of Prague. Their castle is not just the former residence of kings and emperors. Hradčany is a symbol of their independence and autonomy that dates back over 1000 years to the reign of Prince Wenceslas, who was later canonized and became the patron saint of the Czech people. The Czechs have chanted their moving anthem 'Holy Václav, Duke of Bohemia, preserve us and our children!' ever since. It was not by coincidence that the biggest demonstrations of the 'Velvet Revolution' of 1989 were centred around the statue of the prince, seated majestically astride his steed, that dominates the Václavské náměstí (Wenceslas Square). This square, which actually resembles a broad boulevard, has been dubbed by tourists as the 'stomach of Prague' due to its profusion of restaurants, bistros, cafeterias and wine bars. Together with Na příkopě, Ulice 28. října and Národní třída it forms the so-called Zlatý kříž — the Golden Cross. This is a favourite haunt of Prague's young folk, who gather around the café terraces 'by the horse' (the Wenceslas statue). This quarter of the so-called New Town has developed into a centre for international banks, jewellers and hotels. You will probably spot groups of visitors sporting name tags wandering around this area; participants in one of the many international conferences that are held here. The city is reclaiming its position as one of the most important European political and cultural centres.

Prague is attracting increasing numbers of business people and entrepreneurs who have high hopes for the ever improving economic situation. About 60 000 foreign residents, including thousands from America, Britain, Germany and the Netherlands, have been drawn to this city of opportunity where they have set up businesses, cafés and bistros. Unfortunately the Mafia has also now infiltrated this budding young capitalist society, a situation which gives Kafka's words – 'The little mother has claws' – added meaning. But, despite the inevitable problems that a whole new political system brings with it, this great city, once referred to as the 'Paris of the 1920s and 1930s' for its artistic flair and cultural riches, is revelling in a new golden age.

At Vyšehrad Princess Libuše, founder of Prague, stood before the Vltava and prophesied 'I see here a great city, the glory of which will reach to the stars.' Twice in its history Prague has counted among the most famous cities in Europe, but both times the glory has ended in catastrophe. The heyday of Charles IV was followed by the destructive fury of the Hussite Wars, and the prosperous reign of Rudolf II was followed by the Thirty Years War. In both cases a 'defenestration' marked the beginning of the end.

The history of the city on the Vltava is one of constant change. It begins with the afore-mentioned princess Libuše, the progenitrix of the Přemyslid dynasty, who ruled Bohemia from the 9th to the 14th centuries. During the reign of the legendary prince, later Saint, Václav (Wenceslas) (907-935), the land was converted to Christianity, and under Otakar II it developed into a major power. The 'Iron King' was defeated and killed in 1278 by Rudolf of Habsburg, scion of the dynasty, which was to prove a very significant event in the history of Bohemia. Prague basked in a golden age under Charles IV (1346-1378), the son of John of Luxembourg (1310-1346) and Eliška (Elizabeth), the last Přemyslid. He built the Charles Bridge, several Gothic churches, and in 1348 founded the first central European university and the New Town (Nové Město). During the reign of his son, Václav IV, the economic crisis of neighbouring countries extended to Bohemia, and the impoverishment of the people led to the growth of radical movements opposed to the wealthy church. The first European reformer, Jan Hus, was burnt at the stake as a heretic. In 1419 the Hussites threw a number of Catholic councillors from the windows of the New town hall. This 'First Defenestration' marked the beginning of the Hussite Wars (1419-36).

With the marriage of Ferdinand I in 1526, the first Habsburger came to the Bohemian throne. Up to the reign of Rudolf II they were civilized rulers, responsible for many of the city's beautiful buildings. Under Rudolf, Prague became the glittering centre of the empire, and astronomers, artists and alchemists flocked here from all over Europe. But the strife between the Protestant majority and the Catholic minority supported by the Habsburgs increased. After Rudolf's death, the Habsburgs moved to Vienna, and the Bohemian Protestant aristocracy threw the remaining Habsburg governors from the castle windows in 1618 ('the Second Defenestration'). This event sparked off the Thirty Years' War. In 1620, the Protestants lost the Battle of Bílá hora and some 150 000 men, among them the intellectual élite of the country, were forced to abandon their homeland. Bohemia was then attacked by the Swedish Protestants who came to fight the imperial Catholics. The war didn't end in Prague until 1648 when the treaty of Westphalia was signed and the Swedish troops finally left. Bohemia was ruled in absentia by the Habsburgs for another 300 years. The people were forced to reconvert to Catholicism. It was during the

Counter Reformation that some of the greatest Baroque buildings were built.

In the 19th century, a growing national pride led the Czech people to fight for liberty and national recognition until finally, in 1918, the Czechoslovakian Republic was proclaimed. Just 30 years later, however, the Munich Treaty was drawn up and the power of the young republic was handed over to Nazi Germany. Then, after the war, the coup in 1948 brought the Communists to power. In 1968 Alexander Dubček tried to reform the totalitarian state. Soviet tanks brought this attempt at reform, the 'Prague Spring', to a violent end. Twenty years on, the demonstrations of 1988 and the democratic uprising of 1989 finally closed the book on the communist regime. The 'Velvet Revolution' at last restored liberty and democracy.

With the private sector in full expansion and market forces taking root, Prague is reasserting itself. Its streets are once more bustling with commercial activity and café culture. But this new found freedom has resulted in a major historical change: after 74 years of living together as one nation the Czechs and the Slovaks were finally separated in 1993 to form two new republics.

In the Marco Polo Spirit

Marco Polo was the first true world traveller. He travelled with peaceful intentions forging links between the East and the West. His aim was to discover the world, and explore different cultures and environments without changing or disrupting them. He is an excellent role model for the 20th-century traveller. Wherever we travel we should show respect for other peoples and the natural world.

WWF

Exploring the city

Castles and kings, Gothic splendour, princely palaces ...
all the riches of a magical city brought back to life

Most visitors come to Prague for a short two or three day break, which is a shame as this is barely time to scratch the surface of this treasure-filled city. To really explore the most important sights and monuments of the Czech capital you will need a minimum of six days, during which you should make the most of the trams and underground as walking around the hilly terrain can prove exhausting.

A good place to start a tour of Prague is on the Coronation Procession, which leads from the Powder Tower to the Royal Castle. Resist the temptation to dash from one landmark to another in an effort to cram it all in. The best way to really appreciate Prague is to explore it at a leisurely pace. Stop off along the way to the castle and savour a glass of fine Moravian wine in one of the *vinárna* (wine bars) or drop into a *pivnice* (pub) for a cold frothy beer. Take your time, sit

back and look around, relax and absorb the atmosphere.

If, however, you are on a weekend break or you would rather get an overview of the city before exploring its various quarters in greater depth, the guided city tours are a good idea. The bus tour lasts about three hours and will help you get your bearings. It's an unforgettable circuit that escorts you from one historical site to another and it is sure to make your first impression of Prague a lasting one.

As the city is centred around the river, another, perhaps more original, way of seeing Prague is by taking a boat trip along the Vltava. Some of the city's most beautiful buildings are right on the quays.

Prague is built across seven hills, which means there are a number of excellent vantage points offering exceptional panoramas of the city. The view across the sea of towers and domes from the ramp of the Royal Palace, for example, is superb. At midday the air reverberates with the sound of church bells. Banned for so many years

The Charles Bridge with its Baroque statues and the Staré Město bridge tower in the background

these daily chimes are one of the capital's most charming features. The heavy echo of the Sigismund bell, installed in St Vitus Cathedral in 1549, carries for miles and the multitude of bell towers in the town below ring out their response. At exactly midday, the changing of the guard takes place here and the ceremony is accompanied by a brass band. This parade enacted against the backdrop of the city makes for a charming spectacle.

Prague's beauty and charm can also be admired from the top of Petřín Hill, where a miniature version of the Eiffel Tower, originally built for the 1891 Prague Exhibition, still stands. Other wonderful views can be enjoyed from the high Letná plateau, on which the Stalin monument once stood, from Staré Město or Malá Strana bridge towers, and from the Powder Tower on the edge of Staré Město.

Belvedér – Belvedere (D2)

The most beautiful Renaissance building this side of the Alps. A summer palace surrounded by fine arcades, it was built between 1538 and 1564 by Ferdinand I for his wife, queen Anne, to designs by the Genoese architect Paolo della Stella. The bas-reliefs in the columned hall depict hunting scenes, pictures of everyday life and mythological images, as well as a portrayal of the king offering his wife a flower. There is a wonderful view of the castle from the balcony. In the Renaissance garden stands the bronze Singing Fountain by Tomáš Jaroš which dates from 1564. If you crouch down next to the bronze bowls at the base of the fountain, you can hear the musical sounds made by the falling water — hence the fountain's name. The palace itself houses many exhibitions.

MARCO POLO SELECTION: SIGHTSEEING

1 The castle
Majestic symbol of the Czech nation (page 30)

2 The Charles Bridge
Open-air sculpture gallery (page 20)

3 Terrace gardens
The splendid gardens of Prague Castle (page 27)

4 Loreta
Spectacular diamond monstrance (page 16)

5 St Nicholas church
Prague's symbol of High Baroque (page 22)

6 Fred and Ginger
Idiosyncratic building by top US architect (page 19)

7 Kampa
Romantic walks (page 27)

8 The astronomical clock
A procession of mechanical figures announce the hour (page 18)

9 Wenceslas Square
The lively heart of the city (page 30)

10 Old Jewish cemetery
Historic Jewish burial ground (page 21)

The Astronomical Clock at the Old Town Hall, with its hourly procession of apostles

Daily (except Mon), but only during exhibitions, 10.00-18.00 hrs; Mariánkské hradby; Metro: Hradčanská (A)

Karolinum – Charles University (F3)

The oldest university in Central Europe was founded in 1348 by Charles IV and placed under the protection of the patron saint of the nation, St Wenceslas. Initially accommodated in several different monasteries, the four faculties were united under one roof by Wenceslas in 1383, in the Gothic house of the mintmaster Johlin Rothlev. All that remains of the original 14th-century building is the oriel window of the former chapel and an arcade. The façade of the Karolinum was rebuilt in the Baroque style in 1718 by František Maximilian Kaňka. In the courtyard of the university stands a statue of the reformer and university rector Jan Hus, by Karel Lidický. The statue of Charles IV is by Karel Pokorný. In the large lecture hall, where graduation ceremonies take place, a large tapestry hangs on the end wall, depicting *Charles IV kneeling before St Wenceslas* (1947), inspired by a silver seal dating from 1348. The Charles University has played an important role in the history of the nation, and the people of Prague still mourn the loss of the university archives: Charles IV's original charter, the precious Papal Charter and the valuable university insignia all disappeared during the Second World War.

Zelžená ulice; Metro: Můstek (A and B)

Klementinum (E3)

After the Habsburg Ferdinand I had acquired the Kingdom of Bohemia through his wife (1526), he summoned the Jesuits to this overwhelmingly Protestant country. Between 1653 and 1727, under the leadership of Francesco Caratti and František Maximilian Kaňka, they constructed the Klementinum – the largest site in Prague after the Castle itself. Made up of several rather austere buildings erected on a two-hectare site near the Charles Bridge, it was the intellectual bastion of the Counter-Reformation. The complex includes the Vlašská Chapel, the churches of St Clemens and St Salvator, four inner courtyards and an observatory with a tower, the roof of which is crowned with a statue of Atlas. Nowadays it houses the National Library collection, which consists of over

5 million volumes and about 5000 medieval manuscripts. The old refectory, with its monumental paintings and rococo stove, now serves as a reading room.

Entrance Křižovnická, Karlova ulice, nám. Mariánské; Metro: Staroměstská (A)

Královská cesta – Coronation Procession (G3-E3,D3-D2)

The Bohemian Kings were crowned in St Vitus Cathedral. For centuries, they would hold a coronation procession from the Royal Court (which no longer exists, but stood on the site of the Municipal House), by the Powder Tower through the Celetná to the Staroměstské náměstí, and then along Karlova to the Charles Bridge, and up the Nerudova to the castle. The most spectacular of the processions was that of Maria Theresia and Leopold II. Cannons were always fired during these processions, except for that of Frederick V of Pfalz as he was afraid of cannon fire. The last King of Bohemia crowned here was Ferdinand V in 1836. His successor, Franz Josef I, did not keep his promise to be crowned in Prague, and the Czechs have never forgiven him for it.

Metro: Náměstí Republiky (B) or Hradčanská (A)

Loreta (C2)

★ After the defeat of the Protestant army in the Battle of the White Mountain (Bílá hora) in 1620, the victorious Habsburgs wanted the population to re-embrace the Catholic Church. To encourage conversion, beautiful churches and monuments were erected. One of the most outstanding of these was the Loreto, the jewel of the Bohemian Counter-Reformation. At the centre of this sanctuary is the Loreto Chapel, a replica of the Casa Santa de Loreto in Italy. The Prague 'Casa Santa' (Holy House) was commissioned by Princess Lobkovicz and built between 1626 and 1631 by Giovanni Battista Orsi. Inside is a silver altar and a Madonna carved from cedar wood. The Casa Santa is surrounded by a cloister, on the east side of which stands the church. In the Chapel of the Virgin Mary (on the right) is the famous statue of the bearded St Wilgefortis. According to legend this Portuguese princess was to marry the King of Sicily but she did not want to give up her virginity. She prayed to God and he gave her a beard. Upon seeing the princess, the King of Sicily refused to marry her. Her father was so angry that he had her crucified and she became a martyr. The western façade topped with a tower that looks on to the square was built between 1720 and 1722 by Kilian Ignac Dientzenhofer. Every hour the carillon plays a canticle to the Virgin Mary, as it has done for the past 300 years. The vault houses some extraordinary treasures. There are 300 priceless exhibits in all, the most spectacular of which is the diamond monstrance dating from 1698: this holy vessel is studded with 6222 diamonds and weighs 12 kg. To the north of the church there is a little lane that leads to the Nový Svet ('New World'), a picturesque area clustered with artists' cottages.

Daily (except Mon) 09.00-12.00 and 13.00-17.00 hrs; Loretánské náměstí7; Metro: Hradčanská (A)

Obecní dům – Municipal House (G3)

The site of the Municipal House was once occupied by the Royal Court, built by Václav IV, and inhabited by him at the close of the 14th century, when he moved out of Prague Castle. By the 16th century, however, the palace had already fallen into ruin and the building was finally demolished in the early 1900s. The front of the magnificent Art Nouveau Municipal House, built in its place between 1906 and 1911, is adorned with a mosaic entitled *Homage to Prague.* Inside the building are six concert and dance halls, a restaurant and a café. The Smetana Hall provides the stage for the opening concert of the 'Prague Spring' Festival. It was here on the 28th October 1918 that Czechoslovak independence was declared.

Under renovation until May 1997; Náměstí republiky 5; Metro: Náměstí republiky (B)

Prašná brána – Powder Tower (G3)

⚠ The Powder Tower (1475), one of the last vestiges of the old town ramparts, marked the beginning of the Coronation Procession to the Castle. The ornate Gothic decoration was the work of architect and stonemason Matouš Rejsek. At the end of the 17th century, the tower served as a store for gunpowder and it has since become known as the Powder Tower. The view from the top of the 43 m tower over the tiled rooftops and the *vert-de-gris* domes of the Old Town is well worth the climb. Before the Second World War the 'Ladies of the Powder Tower'

were a familiar sight in this area.
Daily, April-August, 09.00-19.00 hrs; Náměstí Republiky; Metro: Náměstí Republiky (B)

Rudolfinum (E2)

On the north side of the *náměstí Jana Palacha* (formerly Red Square) the recently renovated Rudolfinum is a beautiful Neo-Renaissance construction. It was built between 1876 and 1884 by the same architects who designed the National Theatre, Josef Zítek and Josef Schulz. Named after Crown Prince Rudolf, the structure was originally intended to promote art, music, literature and science for Czech-speaking people. The building was inaugurated with a concert conducted by Antonín Dvořák. A large staircase leads to the monumental columned foyer, which in turn leads to the superb Dvořák hall, which features excellent acoustics. The hall holds 1200 spectators and it is here that the closing concert of the Prague Spring Festival — a rendition of Beethoven's Ninth Symphony — is traditionally played. This building also houses an interesting art gallery that displays works from the turn of the century. The balustrade in the foyer features statues of famous artists, composers and writers. The square on which the Rudolfinum stands is named after the philosophy student who set himself alight in Wenceslas Square in 1969 in protest against the Soviet invasion. A bust of him stands in front of the Faculty of Philosophy on the square.
Daily (except Mon) 10.00-18.00 hrs; Café Rudolfinum, entrance from Aleš -Ufer 12 or Palach Square, Metro: Staroměstská (A)

Staroměstská mostecká věž – Staré Město bridge tower (E3)

Built in 1391 according to plans drawn up by Peter Parlers, this is one of the most impressive medieval towers in Europe. Above the Gothic gate you can still make out the coats of arms that represented all the fiefs of the Bohemian kingdom, together with a veil and kingfisher, the symbol of King Wenceslas IV. The statues of the bridge's patrons were also made in Parler's workshop: St Vitus, protector of the bridge is flanked by Charles IV on the right and Wenceslas IV on the left, while above them stand St Sigismund and St Vojtěch (Adalbert). The decorations that were once a feature of the western (river) side of the bridge, were destroyed in 1648 by heavy artillery when the town was besieged by the Swedes.

Daily 09.00-19.00 hrs; Karlův; Karlův most, The Charles Bridge; Metro: Staroměstská (A)

Staroměstská radnice – Old Town Hall (F3)

In 1338, King John of Luxembourg gave the Staré Město permission to build its own town hall. The costs were to be met by the introduction of a new wine tax. The inhabitants must have liked their drink, for within the same year they raised enough funds to acquire an early Gothic corner house. Some years later

the 69 m-high belfry which offers a great view) was added as a symbol of the secular power of the city – as if in defiance of the twin towers of the Týn Church on the other side of the square. On the south side stands ★ the Astronomical Clock (1410) which tells Old Bohemian time and

The Powder Tower in the Old Town (Staré Město)

Changing Money

Banks are generally the best place to change money since the commission charges are only 1-2%. Changing money through private bureaux de change will cost you more as they often charge as much as 4-5% commission.

Babylonian time and standard time. This masterpiece has a highly complex mechanism that indicates the phases of the sun and the moon and their positions as they travel through the zodiac, as well as a famous procession of the Apostles. Every hour, locals and tourists alike gather to admire the parade of mechanical figurines: as the clock strikes, the twelve apostles file out across the top windows, followed by Christ. Below, Death appears holding an hourglass and scythe, sounding the death knell. Then comes a Turk shaking his head in frustration at the failed invasion, followed by the Miser clutching his moneybag and Vanity basking in his own reflection. The end of the show is signalled by the appearance of a cockerel, and the clock chimes the hour. In 1621, 27 Protestant leaders of an uprising against the Catholic Habsburgs were decapitated on the eastern side of the town hall. This was a tragedy for the Kingdom of Bohemia, which lost its independence for the next 300 years.

Mon-Fri 09.00-19.00 hrs, Sat/Sun 09.00-18.00 hrs; the tower 09.00-17.30 hrs, Mon 11.00-17.30 hrs; PIS information desk in the Town Hall; Tel: 24 48 22 02; Staroměstské náměstí; Metro: Staroměstská (A)

Tančící Dům –
Fred and Ginger (E5)

★ Top architect Frank O. Gehry was commissioned by a bank to build this amazing construction. It consists of two intertwining towers made of concrete and glass. The people of Prague have named it after Fred Astaire and Ginger Rogers as it supposedly resembles a couple dancing.

By the river, corner of Resslova and Rašínovo nábřeží; Metro: Karlovo náměstí (B)

U kamenného zvonu –
House at the Stone Bell (F3)

Originally a Romanesque building from the 13th century, it was converted in 1325 into a city residence – probably for Queen Eliška of the Přemyslid dynasty. Until 30 years ago the building still had a Neo-Baroque façade, then it underwent a thorough restoration that uncovered a wealth of Gothic detail beneath, testifying to the building's original splendour. This façade is without equal in Central Europe. Ancient music and modern art exist in harmony in the beautiful halls and chapels. On the left wall of the entrance hall is a statue of the 'Venus with a mocking smile' (as described by Johannes Urzidil), with a globe between her thighs, and her index finger on her lap; originally the frivolous slogan read: 'The Earth revolves around this point'.

During exhibitions daily except Mon, 10.00-18.00 hrs; Staroměstské náměstí 13; Metro: Staroměstská (A)

BRIDGES

Čechův most - The Čech bridge (E2)

The graceful Art Nouveau Čechův most, a continuation of the beautiful Pařížská avenue, was built between 1906 and 1908 and named after a 19th century Czech writer. Of particular interest are the decorative figures that hold the lights, as well as the statue of Victory.

Metro: Staroměstská (A)

Karlův most –
The Charles Bridge (D-E3)

★ ⚘ ❂ The Charles Bridge that links the Old Town to Malá Strana is one of the wonders of Prague. It was built in 1357 to replace the Romanesque Judith Bridge, a wooden structure built towards the end of the 12th century. This magnificent Gothic feat of engineering is the work of Peter Parler, who was awarded the commission by Emperor Charles IV. Resting on 16 columns, it is 520 m long and 10 m wide. The predominantly Baroque statues were added between 1683 and 1714. Artistically, the most valuable among these statues is the one of St Lutgard by Matthias Bernhard Braun (12th statue on the left from the Staré Město tower). It depicts the blind saint and her vision of Christ bowing from the cross. The most popular, fright-ening, and laden with legend is the cruel Turk by Ferdinand Maximilian Brokoff (14th on the left) who is depicted guarding imprisoned Christians. The best known is the bronze statue of St John of Nepomuk, a Jesuit martyr whose likeness appeared on bridges all over Catholic central Europe (8th statue on the right). Between the sixth and seventh columns a cross marks the spot where the saint was thrown into the river 600 years ago. If you stand next to the sculpture of St Cajetán (12th statue on the right), there is a lovely view over Kampa, Prague's 'Little Venice'.

This bridge has played a key role in the country's history on many occasions. Frederick V fled across it in 1620 after his defeat at the White Mountain, and the heads of twelve Protestant nobles kept a grisly watch over the bridge as they hung from the Staré Město bridge tower for ten years following their execution in the Staroměstské náměstí. The people of Prague fought against the Swedes on this site in 1648. In 1848, the year of revolution, barricades were set up here by the revolutionaries, 43 of whom lost their lives. These days all invasions of the bridge are of the tourist variety, and it has become something like Prague's answer to Montmartre's Place du Tertre, lined with hawkers, portrait artists and musicians. The two towers on the Malá Strana side form the gateway to the bridge, with the lower tower predating the bridge – erected in the 12th century, it once formed part of the Judith Bridge fortifications. The taller tower was built in 1464. If you look closely at the sandstone wall on the left, about 3 m up you will notice a number of deep grooves. These were probably made 350 years ago by the Swedes who used the facing to sharpen their halberds.

Viewing tower: Daily April-October 10.00-18.00 hrs, November-March 10.00-17.00 hrs; Karlův most; Metro: Staroměstská (A)

CEMETERIES

Nový židovský hřbitov –
The New Jewish Cemetery (0)

Franz Kafka (1883-1924) and his parents, Hermann and Julia Kafka, are buried here.

Open in summer Thurs-Sat 08.00-20.00 hrs, Sun 09.00-20.00 hrs and in winter Thurs-Sun 09.00-16.00 hrs; Žižkov, Nad vodovodem 1; Metro: Želivského (A)

Starý židovský hřbitov – The Old Jewish Cemetery (E2)

★ This cemetery is one of the most important Jewish burial grounds in the world. The oldest grave dates back to 1439, the most recent is dated 1787. The rather bizarre aspect of the hilly site stems from a shortage of space (the cemetery is only 200 m long), which led to new graves being piled on top of old ones. In parts there are as many as nine graves on top of each other, containing the remains of 200 000 people. The 12 000 tombstones are a mixture of Gothic, Renaissance and Baroque styles. Some of them feature elaborate reliefs in which the name of the deceased is often represented symbolically. Thus the grave of Rabbi Löw – scholar, founder of a Talmudic school and creator of the *Golem* – is marked with a lion, and next to it is a pine cone, a symbol of immortality. Hands raised in blessing signify that the deceased was a member of a rabbinical family; a jug symbolizes that he belonged to the tribe of Levi, etc. As a gesture of respect, visitors to the cemetery lay small stones rather than flowers on the graves, a custom that is presumed to have originated from the desert. If you wish to follow suit, ancient tradition dictates that you should bring the little stones with you. Taking an English-language tour is recommended.

Daily (except Sat) 09.30-18.00 hrs; Tel: 231 03 02; U starého hřbitova 3a; Metro: Staroměstská (A)

Vyšehrad (F6)

◁ From the steep hill of Vyšehrad, Princess Libuše, the mythical founder of the city and progenitrix of the Přemyslid dynasty, predicted a glorious future for the city of Praha (c. 725). This is also purported to be the site where the first Bohemian princes settled during the 11th century – archaeological excavations are ongoing in the area. A Gothic fortress was built here in the 14th century but was destroyed during the Hussite Wars which broke out in the following century. There are records indicating that a Gothic church once stood here too. The castle ruins, the black sandstone (and extensively renovated) church of St Peter and St Paul and the Romanesque rotunda of St Martin can still be seen. After the ease with which the Swedes were able to invade the city at the end of the Thirty Years' War, the people of Prague decided to fortify their city and, at the end of the 17th century, a citadel with Baroque fortifications was built. During the Romantic era, the legendary Vyšehrad regained notoriety as a symbol of Czech independence, with the establishment of a national Slavín cemetery. This is the most prestigious resting place in the country, and many an illustrious Czech is buried here, including the writers Jan Neruda, Karel Čapek and Božena Němcová, the painter Mikoláš Aleš, the composers Bedřich Smetana and Antonín Dvořák, sculptor Josef Myslbek and violinist Jan Kubelík. A listing of the most noteworthy gravesites is available at the entrance next to the church of St Peter and St Paul.

Daily 09.30-17.00 hrs; Soběslavova; Metro: Vyšehrad (C)

Betlémská kaple – Bethlehem Chapel (E3)

❀ This imposing, stark chapel, which could hold a congregation of 3000, was built between 1391 and 1394 for sermons delivered in the Czech language, rather than the traditional Latin. Its most interesting feature was originally not the altar but the pulpit from where the sermons were preached. At the end of the 14th century, when Bohemia was suffering a series of economic crises, the chapel became a popular forum for debate, which was undoubtedly about secular and spiritual power. It was in this chapel, between 1402 and 1413, that the reformist Jan Hus preached vociferously for the re-formation of both the Church and social hierarchy. In 1415, he was condemned as a heretic and burnt at the stake in Constance – an execution that sparked the Hussite Wars. Demolished in the 18th century, the chapel was painstakingly rebuilt in 1953 with the help of the original plans and drawings. The walls are decorated with paintings based on miniatures from the 'Jena Codex'.
Daily 09.00-17.30 hrs; Betlémské náměstí; Metro: Národní třída (B)

Chrám sv Mikuláše – St Nicholas Church (D3)

★ The building of the church of St Nicholas (1703-1756) marked the apogee of Bohemian high Baroque. It became for the Jesuits the symbol of their triumph and jubilation over the country's return to Catholicism. The nave was built with marvellous boldness by Christoph Dientzen-

hofer, the massive cupola was the work of his son Kilian Ignaz and the slender 75m-high bell tower was built by the latter's son-in-law Anselm Lurago. The monumental ceiling fresco above the nave by Jan Lukas Kracker depicts the glorification of St Nicholas and at 1500 sq m it is one of the largest painted ceilings in Europe. The fresco in the cupola portraying the glorification of the Holy Trinity was painted by Franz Xaver Balko. The four enormous statues under the cupola, and the golden statue of Nicholas above the main altar, are the work of the Prague-born Rococo sculptor Ignác Platzer. The church is bursting with hidden treasures. In the first lateral chapel on the left hangs a painting of the Holy Cross by the prominent Baroque painter Karel Škréta. Above the side altar on the left, on which stands the Gothic statue of the Virgin Mary from Foyen in Belgium (brought here from the well-known site of pilgrimage by the Jesuits), is a sculpture by Jan Lukas Kracker. In this figure he has immortalized a certain curious Jesuit who would peer at him from behind a half-open door.
Malostranské náměstí; Metro: Malostranská (A)

Kostel sv Cyrila a Metoděje – Cathedral of St Cyril & Metodeje (E5)

❀ This church was originally built for the Roman Catholics by Kilian Ignaz Dientzenhofer, between 1730 and 1736. Today it belongs to the Orthodox church. During the Second World War, it bore witness to one of Prague's most tragic chapters under Nazi dictatorship. After the assassination in May 1942 of Richard Heydrich, second in command of the SS in the Third Reich after Himmler and *Reichsprotektor* of the Nazi state of Böhmen und Mähren, the seven Czech agents who orchestrated the killing took refuge in the church crypt. Heydrich's tyranny and his threats ('...in Bohemia and Moravia there is no room for Czechs and Germans...') goaded the then London-based Czech government into sending paratroopers to Prague to carry out the assassination. Although the operation itself was successful, the reprisals were great. The Czech agents' hiding place was betrayed and 350 SS troops laid siege to the church for six hours. In the pitched battle 14 SS men were killed and 21 injured; three of the assassins were killed in the fighting and the other four shot themselves in the crypt Immediately after Heydrich's assassination, 2300 Czechs were summarily executed. The crypt was recently declared a national monument to the victims of the *Heydrichiade* and a memorial to reconciliation.

Thurs-Sat 10.00-16.00 hrs; Resslova 9; Tel and Fax: 29 55 95; Metro: Karlovo náměstí (B)

Kostel sv Jakuba – St Jacob's Church (F3)

This originally Romanesque church was destroyed by fire and subsequently rebuilt in Gothic style in 1366. Between 1689 and 1739 it was again transformed, this time in high Baroque style. The imposing interior is decorated with 21 carved high altars featuring paintings by Petr Jan Brandl. Above the main altar hangs the painting *The Matyrdom of St Jacob* by Václav V. Reiner. The colossal tomb of the High Chancellor of Bohemia, Vratislav von Mitrovice (d. 1635) is the most beautiful in Prague. It is worth visiting the church during mass or a concert to fully appreciate the remarkable acoustics. The organ, the largest Baroque organ in Prague, has 4 manuals and 95 registers.

Malá Štupartská 8; Metro: Náměstí Republiky (B)

Kostel Křižovníků – Knights' Church (F3)

Also known as St Francis Church, it was built between 1578 and 1602 for the Knights of the Order of the Cross. An unimpressive entrance leads to a valuable collection of the Order's treasures, also the underground St Francis Chapel, and a well-preserved arch of the Judith Bridge (1167-1342), precursor of the Charles Bridge, on display for the first time in 1995 after centuries of being hidden away.

Křižovnické nám. 3; Metro: Staroměstská (A)

Kostel Panny Marie Sněžné – St Mary of the Snows (F3)

Founded by Charles IV as the Coronation Church in 1347, it was meant to surpass St Vitus Cathedral in size, with a length of more than 100 m. The high, light and breathtaking Presbytery – at 35 m the tallest church building in Prague – was completed in 1397. The actual building was never finished due to the Hussite Revolution. Inside on the left is the highest main altar in Prague (1625), with the painting *The Annunciation* by Václav Vavřinec Reiner and a pewter baptismal font (1459) at the entrance. The church became a centre of the radical wing of the Hussites. In 1419 the priest Jan Želivský gathered a procession of Prague's poorest and marched from Wenceslas Square along the Štěpánská to the Nové Město town hall where the crowd threw the councillors out of the windows, marking the first Prague defenestration. This radical spark lit the flames of the Hussite Revolution (1419-1434).

Jungmannovo náměstí; Metro: Můstek (A)

Kostel P. Marie Vítežné – Church of Panny Maria Victoria (D3)

The earliest Baroque church in Prague (1613) is known around the world, particularly in Italy, Spain, throughout Latin America and the Philippines, for its effigy of the infant Jesus. On the marble altar on the right inner wall hangs the famous wax statue, which originates from Spain. It was presented to the church as a gift from Polyxena of Lobkovicz in 1628. Many miraculous deeds have been attributed to the statue. The infant effigy has over 60 robes from all over the world, a velvet suit with golden embroidery was a gift from (and sewn by) the Empress Maria Theresia herself. The statue may only be dressed by nuns of the resident order – to witness this ceremony is a real experience. The church was given the name 'Victoria' following the victory of the Catholics over the Protestants at the battle of White Mountain (1620).

Karmelitská ulice; Metro: Malostranská (A)

Kostel sv Tomáše – St Thomas' Church (D2)

This beautiful church, with its delicate spire, is not far from the Malá Strana. King Václav II laid the foundation stone in 1285 for the church and its monastery. The building was completed by the Augustine hermits in early Gothic style in 1379. The monastery was very rich, since the monks had been operating a brewery here since 1358. For nearly 600 years they brewed excellent black beer, using ancient recipes. In 1637 the prior J. Svitavský commissioned Peter Paul Rubens to paint two pictures – *The Death of St Thomas* and *St Augustine*. The originals now hang in the National Gallery, while the church exhibits copies. The church was rebuilt in Baroque style by Kilian Ignaz Dientzenhofer between 1723 and 1731, the magnificent interiors were created by renowned Bohemian artists and the main altar is by Kristián Kovář. The ceiling frescos are by Václav V. Reiner and the two large statues on the main altar are the work of Jan A. Quitainer. Around the corner in Tomášská Lane is a Baroque house (no 4), also by Dientzenhofer, which displays one of the finest house signs in Prague – *St Hubertus with a deer* – by Ferdinand Maximilian Brokoff.

Letenská ulice; Metro: Malostranská (A)

Týnský chrám – Týn Church (F3)

✤ With its two 80 m-high towers and sumptuous ornamentation, the Týn Church is one of the most important monuments of the Bohemian Gothic period. Built between 1365 and 1511, it

became the headquarters of the Prague Utraquists – moderate Hussites – who practised holy communion 'in both forms' (bread and wine) whence their choice of the chalice as a symbol. The giant, heavily gilded chalice, which held 400 litres and which the Hussite king Jiří z Poděbrad had placed next to his statue in the high stone gable, was melted down in the 17th century and its gold was reworked into a statue of the Virgin Mary. The beautiful tympanum over the north portal depicts scenes from Christ's Passion. In the gloomy interior it is worth keeping an eye out for the Gothic Madonna and Child on the wall of the right aisle (c. 1400), the late Gothic stone baldaquin by Matouš Rejsek (1493), the painting of *The Assumption* by Karel Škréta (on the main altar), and, to the right in front of the main altar, the marble gravestone of the Dane Tycho Brahe, Emperor Rudolf II's astronomer, who lost his nose in a duel. The north and south apses feature Gothic benches with corbels in the form of the heads of King Václav IV and his wife.
Staroměstské náměstí; Metro: Staroměstská (A)

PALACES

Černínský palác – Černín Palace (C2-3)

Count Humprecht Jan Černín z Chudenic, the wealthy imperial ambassador in Venice, decided to build a palace in Prague which he could boast of to all the nobility of Europe. He chose the reputed architect Francesco Caratti, who constructed the 150 m-long building with its 30 grandiose half-columns between 1668 and 1688. There is one story that encapsulates the Count's desperate quest for prestige: in September 1673, Emperor Leopold I was expected for the laying of the foundation stone of St Nicholas Church. Černín urged his architect to speed up the building process so that he could show the Emperor the greatest building ever constructed north of the Alps. Instead of being impressed, the Emperor was insulted, as the Count had thus outshone his own royal castle in Vienna. The count invested 100 000 florins in the first phase of building alone – no one knows what the final bill amounted to. In 1742 the French army plundered the palace and in 1757 the Prussians severely damaged it during a heavy bombardment. In the early years of the Czechoslovak Republic (1928-34) the palace was reconstructed, and it became the seat of the Foreign Ministry. Since then it has not been spared the irony of the locals: one tourist was heard to ask, 'How many people work in this building?', to which a local replied 'About half of them'.
Loretánské náměstí 5; Metro: Hradčanská (A) and tram 22

Lichtenštejnský palác – Liechtenstein Palace (E3)

The Queen and the Duke of Edinburgh stayed here during their official visit in March 1996. Royal connections go back to the time of Charles IV (1346-78) whose daughter, Princess Anna, married the English King Richard II and became known as 'Good Queen Ann'. The palace houses a concert hall, gallery and a café.
Kampa; Metro: Malostranská (A)

Lobkovický palác –
Lobkovic Palace (D3)

Looking southwards from the castle parapet, you can make out the upper section of the Lobkovic Palace, built at the beginning of the 18th century in early Baroque style by Giovanni Batista Alliprandi. In 1753, it came into the possession of the Lobkovic family, who laid out a large English garden behind it. When it later housed the West German embassy, the palace gardens were used as a refuge for thousands of East German citizens, who abandoned their Trabants and Wartburgs in the neighbouring streets. A Czech artist painted one of these 'Trabis' in gold, fitted it with long legs and placed it in the Lobkovic Gardens. In memory of these events the German foreign minister unveiled a plaque here in October 1994.

Vlašská 19; Metro: Malostranská (A)

Morzinský palác –
Morzin Palace (D3)

The steep lane of Nerudova is not only notable for its house signs – such as 'The Golden Cups', 'The Ass at the Manger', 'The Red Lion' and 'The Two Suns' – but also for the Morzin Palace. Its architectural design by Giovanni Santini and the sculpture by Ferdinand Maximilian Brokoff make this one of the finest palaces in Prague. The balcony is supported by two Moors, representing the heraldic motif of the Morzin family. Over the doorway are two busts: one representing night and the other, day. The balustrade is decorated with allegorical figures of the four continents. Australia had not yet

been discovered when the palace was built in 1713-14.

Nerudova ulice 5; Metro: Malostranská (A)

Palác Kinských –
Kinský Palace (F3)

This beautiful palace in the Staroměstské náměstí was built between 1755 and 1765 in late Baroque style. It combines unusual Rococo elements by Anselm Lurago inspired by the designs of Kilian Ignaz Dientzenhofer, the architect of the church of St Nicholas opposite. From 1786 to 1945 the palace belonged to the Counts Kinský. A balcony, supported by two colonnaded doorways, runs across almost the entire front of the building. Countess Berta Kinský, the first woman to win the Nobel Peace Prize (1905) was born here. The palace was also home to the Kafka family, during its time as the Austro-Hungarian Imperial *Deutsche Altstädter Gymnasium*, when the young Franz attended the school. The rooms on the ground floor on the south-west side of the building housed the shop 'Hermann Kafka, Wholesale Haberdashers'. During the Czechoslovak Republic the salesman bohemianized his name to Heřman. Today the palace contains the graphic art collection of the National Gallery, which comprises around 150 000 items. It frequently hosts exhibitions.

Staroměstské náměstí 12; Metro Staroměstská (A)

Smiřických palác –
Smiřický palace (D3)

At the end of the 16th and beginning of the 17th centuries, Europe was like a time bomb waiting to explode. In almost every country, there were violent clashes between Catholics and Protestants. The continent was divided into two powerful ideological blocks, the Catholic League and the Protestant Union. The Kingdom of Bohemia, in which 90% of the population were Protestant, was a prime example of a central European corporative state, ruled by a Protestant aristocracy. However, their rights were restricted by the two Catholic governors in the Bohemian Chancellery, representatives of the Catholic emperor in Vienna. On 22nd May 1618, Protestant leaders met at the Smiřický palace and decided to dispose of the imperial governors – Counts Martinic and Slavata – in Prague Castle. The day after the meeting Protestants marched to the Bohemian Chancellery and threw the governors out of the 16 m- high windows (the Second Prague Defenestration). This uprising of the Bohemian Protestants sparked off the Thirty Years' War.

Malostranské náměstí 18; Metro: Malostranská (A)

PARKS & GARDENS

Františkánská zahrada (F4)

The peaceful monastery gardens of St Mary of the Snows were laid out at the same time as the New Town (1348). Since the beginning of the 17th century the whole estate has belonged to the Franciscan friars. The gardens have recently been decorated with stylish lamps and lovely sculptures: the lovely *Davídek* (little David) portrays the natural power of water, three nymphs float on the surface, and a bust of

the legendary Aesop stands on the ground nearby. The high chancel of the church is particularly impressive when viewed from the gardens.

Metro: Můstek (A and B)

Hradní terasovité zahrady – Castle Terrace Gardens (D2)

★ The jewel in the crown of Prague's gardens. The Ledebour and smaller Palffy gardens were re-opened in 1995 with the assistance of a special foundation set up under the patronage of Prince Charles and President Václav Havel. The enchanting Sala Terrena designed by F. M. Kaňka in the early 18th century, today provides a wonderful venue for chamber music concerts.

Daily 10.00-22.00 hrs; Valdštejnská 162; Metro: Malostranská (A)

Hradní zahrady – Castle Gardens (D2)

The gardens can be reached via the Bull Staircase, designed by Plečnik, who also remodelled the rampart gardens. The huge granite bowl in the Paradise Garden is worth seeing, as is the viewing terrace of the South Garden. Underneath the so-called Ludwig Wing, two obelisks mark the spot where Counts Slavata and Martinic, the two Habsburg governors who were victims of the 'Second Defenestration' in 1618, landed on the dung heap.

Metro: Hradčanská (A)

Kampa (E3)

★ ◁╲╱ The romantic island of Kampa is separated from Malá Strana by a small strip of water, known as Čertovka (the devil's stream). On the northern side of the Charles Bridge, the Čertovka

flows past a small cluster of houses – this is the 'Little Venice' of Prague. This peaceful island is the perfect place for a quiet stroll through the gardens and offers enticing views over the Vltava, the Charles Bridge and the National Theatre. If you are lucky, you might catch a glimpse of a flock of swans swimming on the other side of the river.
Metro: Malostranská (A)

Královská zahrada – Royal Gardens (D2)

An Italian gardener named Francesco designed these beautiful Renaissance gardens in 1535 for Emperor Ferdinand I. Besides the magnificent flowers and some exotic plants, the first tulips in Europe were cultivated here by the Emperor's personal physician and botanist, P. O. Mathioli. Originally built in 1569 for ball games, the Míčovna, richly decorated with fine sgraffito, was later used for parties, masked balls and plays. It has recently been turned into an art gallery. The delightful *Allegory of the Night* in front of the Míčovna comes from the workshop of Matthias Braun. Rudolf II had animal cages erected in the Lion court. On the way to the Belvedere, there is a Baroque niche with a fountain and statue of Hercules (1670). In the 19th century, the garden was transformed into an English style landscape and now, after many years, it is once again open to the public.
Daily 10.00-17.45 hrs; Hradčany; Metro: Hradčanská (A)

Valdštejnský palác – Valdštejn Palace (D2)

The largest and most splendid palace in Prague was built be-tween 1623 and 1630 by the Generalissimo of the imperial army Albrecht Wenzel von Waldstein (the Wallenstein of Schiller's trilogy). His palace was intended as a counterpoint to Prague Castle. Wallenstein's power was so great that he aspired to the throne of Bohemia, so the emperor had him killed in the town of Cheb. The extensive gardens are laid out in *sala terrena* style, unique in central Europe at the time. A vast loggia opens out to the gardens and the paths are decorated with bronze statues by Adrian de Vries. These are actually copies; the originals were taken by the Swedes at the end of the Thirty Years' War (1648). There is a good view of the castle from the park.
Gardens, daily May-Sept 09.00-19.00 hrs; Letenská ulice; Metro: Malostranská (A)

Vrtbovská zahrada – Vrtba Gardens (D3)

These charming gardens laid out in 1725 are soon to be reopened after lengthy renovation. To enter you will pass through a doorway and under an archway. You then climb uphill through a lovely Baroque garden (designed by F. M. Kaňka), scattered with jolly cherubs, vases and statues by Matthias Braun. Right at the top there is an observation terrace which offers an unusual view of Mála Strana.
Karmelitská 27, Metro: Malostranská (A)

SQUARES

Křižovnické náměstí – Knights' Square (E3)

The Church of St Francis Seraphikus (on the left of the

The Jan Hus Memorial on the Staroměstské náměstí commemorates the great medieval reformer (1369-1415)

Charles Bridge), the Church of St Salvator and the Staré Město bridge towers form a small but picturesque square. A memorial to Charles IV, the founding charter in hand, was erected here to mark the 500th anniversary of the foundation of the Charles University. Designed by the Burgundian architect Mathey, the green-domed Knights' Church (see page 23) was built between 1679 and 1689. Christoph Willibald Gluck and Antonín Dvořák worked here as organists. Opposite the Charles Bridge stands the Renaissance church of St Salvator by Francesco Caratti and Carlo Lurago, with its Baroque portal (1572-1602) and twin towers, which were added later, designed by František Maximilian Kaňka. Peter Parler's Gothic bridge tower, often called the finest in Europe, completes the square. There is always something going on here: a wind

quartet playing Baroque music, or a group of young people playing rhythmic jazz.
Metro: Staroměstská (A)

Staroměstské náměstí – Old Town Square (F3)

◈ This square has been an important commercial and political market-place since the 12th century, when foreign merchants first convened on this 'crossroads to Bohemia' from the West and the South. Behind the Týn church in the Ungelt (literally, 'No Money') these purveyors would pay duty on their goods and offer them for sale. Prague is often referred to as the city of tragedy, since its cobblestones have been steeped in blood – the most notorious of several bloody events took place on 21st June 1621 when, after a failed uprising against the Habsburgs, 27 Bohemian and German noblemen and citizens were executed in

front of the Town Hall. On the pavement, the spot where they fell is marked with 27 crosses. This event sealed Habsburg control over Bohemia for another 300 years. Jousting also took place in the square and to the delight of the spectating citizens, King Jan Lucemburský was once unseated here. A likeness of the great reformer Jan Hus, flanked by the oppressed and the defiant, looks from his immense memorial towards the Týn church, where the first reformation struggles began. The Gothic palace 'House at The Stone Bell', with its beautiful façade, was home to the Přemyslid Eliška, heiress to Bohemia and mother of Charles IV. The magnificent coronation processions of the Bohemian kings would cross this square and march up to St Vitus Cathedral for the conferring of the royal title. The square has been impressively renovated; tourists stream to the town hall to admire the Astronomical Clock's hourly Parade of the Apostles (from 08.00-20.00 hrs). In fine weather, visitors can immerse themselves in the wonderful ambience of these historical buildings as they sit under the colourful café umbrellas. During his stay in Prague from 1910-1911, Einstein presented his theory of relativity at number 18, which was then a literary salon run by Berta Fanta and frequented by Kafka and others – it is now occupied by Café Amadeus.
Metro: Staroměstská (A)

Václavské náměstí –
Wenceslas Square (F-G3-4)
★ ☼ Originally, this 750 m-long and 60 m-wide area was a horse market. It represented a classic example of urban planning under Charles IV. Today it is more like an elegant boulevard than a square, and in recent history it has become something of a political seismograph for the nation. Lined with hotels, cinemas, restaurants, cafés and businesses, the square forms what is known as the Golden Cross, with the Na příkopě (jokingly called Prague's Wall Street due to its profusion of banks), Na Můstku, 28. října and Národní třída. At the top end of the square is the vast National Museum, in front of which stands the statue of Prince Václav, after whom the square is named, escorted by the equestrian statues of the national saints Ludmilla, Procopius, Agnes and Adalbert of Prague (by Vojtěch). It was near this monument in 1969 that Jan Palach committed suicide by setting himself alight, in protest at the Soviet occupation. The protests against the Communist regime were also concentrated around this square and it is here that the democratic revolution began.
Metro: Můstek (A and B), Muzeum (A and C)

★ ⚐ ☼ **(D2)** For more than 1000 years Prague Castle has been at the centre of the country's political life. The Guinness Book of Records has classed it as the biggest castle in the world. It covers an area of 7.2 hectares, is 570 m long and 128 m wide. For over 1000 years too, this has been the secular and spiritual heart of Bohemia, and its every stone seems to retain a little piece of history. Founded in about 880

The 'Battling Titans' by Ignác Platzer adorn the castle gates

AD, the Castle was built in the Romanesque style by the Přemyslids, and transformed by successive dynasties – into Gothic by the Luxembourg princes, Late Gothic by the Jegiellons, and Renaissance and Baroque by the Habsburgs. The last rebuilding work (1753-1775) gave the castle its current Classical form. After the founding of the Czechoslovak Republic in 1918 the castle once again became a symbol of statehood, and the presidential headquarters. In 1989, poet and former state enemy number one Václav Havel became president and took up residence here.

It is worth hiring a guide to the castle; information is available in the second courtyard Chapel of the Holy Cross. Tel: 33 37 33 68

The Castle

The main entrance is on the Hradčanské náměstí, through gates decorated with two 'Battling Titans' by the sculptor Ignác Platzer, into the main courtyard where the changing of the guard (12.00 hrs) is worth seeing. Above the equally monumental Baroque Matthias Gate (1614) to the right

the presidential flag, bearing the state coat of arms and Hussite slogan *Pravda vitezí* ('Truth Prevails'), flies when the president is in residence. In the middle of the second courtyard is a Baroque fountain carved from sandstone. The beautifully appointed Spanish Hall (1601-06), which once held part of the famous art collection belonging to Rudolf II, is open to the public for concerts – as is the Belvedere. The castle's art gallery displays what remains of the royal art collection, with about 70 paintings by Rubens, Titian, Veronese, Tintoretto and Kupecky, among other illustrious artists. At the opposite end of the castle, seven rooms are given over to the permanent exhibition of toys from the Ivan Steiger collection *(daily 09.30-17.30 hrs)*. Since 1993 the Theresia wing (1766-1768), which had been residential, has been open to the public. At the north entrance, to the left behind the Pacassi gate, are the Imperial Stables (dating from the early 16th century), also newly opened as an exhibition and concert centre. About 150 m north of here, in the Lví dvůr (Lion Court), Rudolf II had animal cages built to hold lions, tigers and bears. The royal astronomer Tycho Bryhe prophesied that the ailing emperor would expire shortly after his favourite lion. Prophesy became reality – the ruler died two days after the animal. The site is now a restaurant.

Katedrála sv Víta
St Vitus Cathedral

❖ To build the perfect setting for the coronation and burial of Bohemian kings, Charles IV called in two brilliant architects,

St Vitus Cathedral, coronation church for the Bohemian kings

the Frenchman Matthias of Arras and, after his death in 1352, Peter Parler. Construction began in 1344, and was interrupted by the beginning of the Hussite War in 1420. During this time, only the chancel and the foundations of the main tower were built. ❧ The 99 m-high tower, which houses the Sigismund Bell (1549) – at 17 000 kg it is the biggest church bell in Bohemia – was built in Gothic style and finished in Renaissance and Baroque style. One of the jewels of Gothic architecture in Prague is the Triforium (1371-75), which runs right round the chancel. Following a design by Peter Parler, it consists of 21 busts of royal family members sculpted after sketches by Peter Parler, including Charles IV and his four wives and son Václav IV, as well as those who had performed some service in the construction of the cathedral. All project a fascinating

vibrancy. Closed for decades, the gallery is now open *(for an appointment ring 33 37 33 68)*. The cathedral is 124 m long, 60 m wide and 34 m high and was finally completed to Parler's original plans in 1929.

Chapel of St Václav

One of the most revered spots in the cathedral is the Chapel of St Václav (Wenceslas), the heart of the cathedral, and the high point of Bohemian Gothic art. Peter Parler built it between 1362 and 1364 on the site where, in the original St Vitus rotunda, the Přemyslid prince Václav was buried. The walls are completely covered in gold leaf and over 1300 semi-precious gems, arranged around 14th century Gothic frescos portraying Christ's passion and, above this, scenes from the Václav legend, work of the Litomerice school. On a ledge above the altar stands a Gothic statue of St Wenceslas (1373).

Coronation Chamber

Above the Chapel lies the Coronation Chamber, which serves as the treasury of the Bohemian crown jewels. The chamber door is fitted with seven locks that can only be opened by the seven holders of the keys – including the president and the speaker of parliament – acting in concert. The crown is encrusted with 91 gems, which include numerous emeralds, six enormous sapphires, and 20 pearls, and weighs 2360 g. A replica of the crown jewels is on show at the Historical Exhibition in the Lobkovíc Palace, not far from Golden Lane.

Imperial Mausoleum and Choir

In front of the high altar in the chancel is the white marble Renaissance sarcophagus (1564-81), with three figures – Ferdinand I, his wife Anna and their son Maximilian II. The carved wooden relief panelling (1630) on either side of the altar shows the flight of Frederick V after his defeat at the Battle of the White Mountain and the plundering of the cathedral by Calvinists in 1619. To the right of the altar is the magnificent 3 700 kg solid silver tomb of St John of Nepomuk, built (1733-36) from extravagant designs by Fischer von Erlach. The Zlatá Brána (Golden Gate) leads back to the third courtyard, where the Gothic bronze statue (1373) of St George stands. The front wall of the cathedral is decorated with a splendid 14th century Gothic mosaic (84 sq m) of the *Last Judgement* (1370-71).

Royal Crypt

The Royal Crypt contains the sarcophagi of Charles IV and his four wives, as well as Václav IV, Rudolf II, Ladislaus Posthumus and Jiří Poděbradys.

Basilika sv Jiří –
Basilica of St George

The Basilica of St George is the oldest and best preserved Romanesque church in Bohemia. It was founded in 920 by Prince Vratislav I and dedicated in 925 as the burial chapel of St Ludmilla. Fifty years later a Benedictine convent was founded here; its abbess was Princess Mlada, sister of King Boleslav II, and all the abbesses who followed were also of royal or aristocratic lineage. On the front wall of the nave are the gravestones of the Přemyslid rulers Vratislav and Boleslav, and in the chapel is the grave of St Ludmilla. Don't miss the 12th-century crypt under the staircase. The convent is now home to the National Gallery's Bohemian Gothic and Baroque collections.

Bohemian Chancellery

In the Ludvíc Wing next to the Vladislav Hall are the rooms of the Bohemian Chancellery, where, in 1618, following a brief argument, the Protestant nobles defenestrated the two imperial governors and their secretary Fabricius. A dung heap allegedly saved them. Fabricius was later honoured somewhat ironically by the emperor in 'a flight of fancy'. This famous 'Second Prague Defenestration' marked the beginning of the Bohemian uprising and led to the Thirty Years' War.

Bilá věž –
The White Tower

A notorious state prison, the White Tower held such prisoners as the English magician E. Kelley and the imperial valet K. Rucky, who hanged himself with the same gold rope used to hang up the key to the imperial treasury (to which the disloyal servant had been granting himself liberal access). Today, it houses an extensive glass exhibition. A permanent display in the Mihulka tower shows an alchemist's kitchen from the time of Rudolf II. It also features the golden vase in which the king's brain was kept.

Černá věž –
The Black Tower

The Black Tower which stands at the end of Golden Lane dates from the first half of the 12th century. Charles IV had the rooftops of the Black and White Towers covered with gold foil, so that they would gleam over the city, possibly giving rise to the name 'The Golden City'.

Vladislavský sál – Vladislav Hall

The beautiful Vladislav Hall in the former Royal Palace is well worth a visit. The 62 m-long, 16 m-wide and 13 m-high hall was built between 1493 and 1502 by Benedikt Ried. With its sweeping rib vaulting, it is the most grandiose hall of the late medieval period – its windows, however, are in early Renaissance style. This is where the Bohemian kings received homage from their vassals, and where coronation festivities complete with jousting events were held. Nowadays, it is where the president takes the oath of office. Note also the Gothic curve of the flat-stepped staircase that served as the entrance for participants in the jousting events. Below the hall is a 14th-century Gothic room named after the Emperor Charles.

Zlatá ulička – Golden Lane   (D-E2)

This picturesque blind alley is one of the most popular sights in Prague. It has also been called Alchemists' Alley since legend has it that the alchemists who lived in these little cottages used to produce the philosophers' stone, the elixir of life and, above all, gold for the Emperor Rudolf II. In fact, it was the bowmen of the castle guards who resided here, followed later by gold-smiths. One of the houses (no. 22) served as a temporary refuge for Franz Kafka in 1917 while he was writing his short stories. A little further down (at no. 14) lived the clairvoyant Madame de Thebe (whose real name was Matylda Prošová), who prophesied the Nazi defeat and was beaten to death by the Gestapo during an interrogation.

Castle walls April-October daily 05.00-24.00 hrs, Buildings daily 09.00-17.00 hrs; Foreign language guides: second courtyard in the Chapel of the Holy Cross; Tel: 33 37 33 68; Metro: Hradčanská (A)

DISTRICTS

Malá strana – Little Quarter   (D3-4)

The Little Quarter is situated on the left bank of the Vltava, in the triangle between the river and the two hills of Hradčany and Petřín, on the slopes below the Castle. The original small settlement of artisans and tradesmen was established in 1257 by Přemyslid King Otakar II as Prague's second town after Staré Město. Many battlements were constructed including the 'Hunger Wall', built under the Strahov Gardens in 1360 by Charles IV. Merchants, who became wealthy from their dealings with the royal court, and the German nobility who came here after their victory in the Battle of the White Mountain gave the Little Quarter its architectural harmony. Next to the green-domed St Nicholas Church, the crowning achievement of Prague Baroque style, are the Baroque palaces of Valdštejn, Nostic, Buquoy, Thun, Furstenberg and

Liechtenstein, all clustered at the foot of the Castle. Many bourgeois Baroque houses, with emblems indicating the profession of their former occupants, add to the picturesque quality of these streets. Some of the palaces became state offices when the Czechoslovak Republic was formed in 1918; others now serve as foreign embassies. The West German Embassy in the Lobkovic Palace hit the headlines in 1989 when thousands of East German citizens sought refuge there. The Little Quarter is famed for its lovely old wine bars, which also serve delicious meals. You can wander around this quarter for hours, view Kampa island, or relax in the tranquil surroundings of the Strahovská or Seminářská gardens.

Metro: Malostranská (A)

Nové město –
New town   (G2-4)

What is still known as the New Town was in fact founded by Charles IV nearly 650 years ago (1348). This semi-circular belt encloses the heart of the old city. The 3 km-long town walls were completed in two years, thus tripling the size of the city. Three massive market squares were laid out: the Horse Market (today Václavské náměstí – Wenceslas Square), the Cattle Market (Karlovo náměstí) and the Hay Market (Senovážné náměstí). Large streets were built 17 to 27 m wide, and the area also has some delightful Gothic churches and monasteries. Building was encouraged through tax concessions – houses built within 18 months of land allocation remained tax free for 12 years. The New Town

bears witness to the genius of the imperial planners, since the medieval city's infrastructure is today able to withstand the demands of a modern city while remaining virtually unchanged.

Metro: Muzeum (A and C).

Staré město –
Old Town   (E-F3-4)

The Old Town is the heart of Prague and reveals much about the historical and architectural development of the city. About 1000 years ago, the Staroměstské náměstí was nothing more than a market square. Then in 1230 King Václav I granted tradesmen and craftsmen the right to build their homes around it and settlements were soon formed. At the time there were already over 40 Romanesque churches in Prague. Charles IV built some Gothic churches in the Old Town and in 1348 founded the first university in Central Europe here. Renaissance and Baroque buildings later appeared and many of the existing Romanesque and Gothic houses were redisigned by architects. Although the Old Town appears a little grey it has nevertheless kept its original charm and coherence of style. The historic buildings are interspersed here and there with modern ones such as the Cubist Dům U černé Matky boží (House of the Black Madonna), on Celetná 34, built in 1911 by Josef Gočár. At the turn of the century the Jewish Quarter, Josefov, was 'sanitized'; fortunately, some of its beautiful monuments were spared. The fine Art Nouveau street of Pařížská is now lined with airline offices and luxury shops, while many of the old houses along the

Coronation Procession, Celetná and Husova have been converted into charming wine cellars.

Metro: Staroměstská (A)

Židovské město – Josefov (E-F2)

Over 1000 years ago, Jewish merchants settled in Prague – all other occupations except trade were forbidden them. A Jewish settlement was first established in the area around the Old Synagogue during the 13th century. The term 'ghetto' first came into use in the 16th century. The settlement became a town, with separate Jewish administration, and synagogues and schools were built. The community repeatedly fell prey to pogroms, most of which were provoked by the Catholic Church. The tolerant Emperor Rudolf II cultivated contact with the Jewish community; in 1592, he met with Rabbi Löw to discuss the secrets of astrology and mysticism. On several occasions, the exceedingly wealthy banker Mordechai Maisel lent the Emperor money for the war against the Turks and to enrich the imperial collections, through which the Emperor earned Prague the title of 'Art Capital of Europe'. At the end of the 19th century Josefov was renovated, old houses torn down and new ones built in their place. Jews were officially granted citizenship in 1848, after which time they could reside in other parts of the city. The old Jewish cemetery, the town hall, and six synagogues survived the renovation. The cemetery is worth a visit and the synagogues now house some exceptional art collections, both religious and secular. These include some fabulous silver artefacts, a collection of tabernacle curtains and scrolls of the Torah from synagogues in Bohemia and Moravia pillaged by the Nazis, who intended to found a 'Museum of an Extinct Race'. During the Second World War, the Jewish community was virtually annihilated and today there are only around a thousand Jewish residents in Prague. The 'Jewish Museum' shows the extent to which the Jewish community contributed to culture and science.

Metro: Staroměstská (A)

THEATRES

Laterna magika (E4)

Next to the National Theatre stands the glass-fronted Nová Scéna theatre (built 1977-83), home to the reputed Laterna Magika company whose performances combine theatre, film, mime, dance and comedy. The Laterna Magika claims its roots can be traced to the late 16th century, during the reign of Rudolf II. Rabbi Löw – theologian, cabbalist and creator of the mythical Golem – is said to have put on a show for Emperor Rudolf II in a darkened room using silhouettes of biblical patriarchs which were so lifelike, many thought they were real. The first Laterna Magika show (under the direction of Alfred Radok), performed at the World Expo in Brussels in 1958, was a resounding success.

Nová scéna, Národní třída 4; Tel: 24 91 41 29; Metro: Národní třída (B)

Národní divadlo – National Theatre (E4)

The Neo-Renaissance National Theatre – known affectionately

among the Czechs as 'The Golden Chapel on the Vltava', is probably the only theatre which was not built by the state, the city, or by the ruling élite. It was built from funds donated by the entire Czech population, including the very poorest, who collected their pennies for several decades to build themselves a National Theatre base. It was designed by Josef Zítek, but tragedy struck when, shortly after construction was completed in 1881, a fire broke out and almost completely destroyed the building. In just 47 days Prague's citizens joined forces once more to collect over one million florins, and two years later the theatre was officially opened. The greatest artists of the age contributed to the decor, both internal and external. To date, the theatre has presented almost 2500 performances of Smetana's opera *Libuše.* The National Theatre also stages ballet.
Národní třída 2; Tel 24 91 26 73; Metro: Národní třída (B)

Státní opera Praha – Prague State Opera (G4)

The neo-classical theatre was built in 1886-7 by the Viennese architects Helmer and Fellner. It was opened in 1888 as the New German Theatre and its inaugural performance was Wagner's *Die Meistersinger.* At the front of the building, images of Dionysius and the muse Thalia stand above busts of Goethe, Schiller and Mozart. The interior is velvet and gold with beautiful plasterwork and decoration. The first complete performance of Wagner's *Ring* was also staged here. The building was renamed

the Smetana Theatre in 1945 and is now the State Opera.
Wilsonova 4; Tel: 24 22 76 93-6 and 24 22 98 98; Metro: Muzeum (A and C)

Stavovské divadlo – Estates Theatre (F3)

The neo-classical Estates Theatre was built in 1781-3 as a forum for entertaining the influential German community. Sixteen years later the Bohemian Estates took it over and renamed it. Mozart chose this theatre for the premières of his operas *The Abduction from the Seraglio* and *The Marriage of Figaro*, to resounding success. He later wrote 'since the people of Prague understand opera so well, I will write one just for them'. In the same year, on 29th October, the theatre staged the premiere of Mozart's new opera, *Don Giovanni*, dedicated to the people of Prague. In January 1792, the theatre mourned the death of the illustrious composer, and held a memorial performance starring his great admirer, the singer Josefina Dušková. Not surprisingly, Milos Forman chose this theatre as a primary location for his award-winning film *Amadeus.* It was also the venue for the first Czech opera *Dráteník* by František Škroup, who was a director in the Estates Theatre from 1827 to 1857. Between 1918 and 1938 both German and Czech performances were staged here, but in the Second World War, only German was permitted. After the war the building was renamed the Tyl Theatre after the composer of the national anthem.
Ovocný trh 6; Tel: 24 21 43 39; Metro: Můstek (A and B)

Cultural riches

*The extensive Prague art collections include Bohemian Gothic,
Dürer's 'Rosenkrantzfest', the diamond monstrance, nineteen
Picassos and other Cubist works*

Each year more than five million people flock to Prague's great museums and art galleries. The Šternberk Palace alone welcomes one million tourists annually and the same number visit the Jewish Museum in the Staré Město. But no trip to Prague is complete without seeing the modern art collection at the National Gallery, which reopened in 1995 after lengthy renovation. An extensive collection of 19th- and 20th-century French art is displayed here alongside the work of Czech and other European artists of the 20th century. The National Museum and National Technical Museum also attract many visitors. Considering that the city has played, and continues to play, such a fundamental role in the history and development of music, there are several interesting museums dedicated to Mozart, Smetana and Dvořák which deserve to be seen. The Strahov Monastery Library, with its historic rooms, is

a fascinating place, while a traditional exhibition venue is the Gothic tower U kammeného zvonmu ('The Stone Bell') on Staroměstské náměstí. More recently, art exhibitions have been held in the Míčovna in the Royal Gardens. The exhibition of old Bohemian art in St George's Monastery behind St Vitus Cathedral is worth a visit, especially for its Gothic masterpieces; if you prefer something more modern, a unique collection of Cubist furniture dating from the turn of the century to the 1920s is housed in the Crafts Museum. For a better understanding of Jewish religion and culture, take the guided tour of the Jewish Museum. English-speaking guides can be hired by the hour or by the day (hourly rates range from about 50 to 100Kč). Information and details of special exhibitions are available from the PIS. All the museums are open every day except Mondays. *PIS: Mon-Fri 09.00-19.00 hrs, Sat/Sun 09.00-17.00 hrs; Na příkopě 20; Tel: 26 40 23; Metro: Můstek (A and B), and in the Old Town Hall; Tel: 24 48 22 02; Metro: Staroměstská (A)*

*The National Museum in Wenceslas
Square is a symbol of the Czech
national renaissance.*

Anežský klášter –
St Agnes Convent (Museum
of 19th century Czech art) **(F2)**
The early Gothic convent of the order of the Poor Clares was founded in 1233 by the devout Czech princess St Agnes, daughter of the Přemyslid king Otakar I, who became its first abbess. After long and painstaking restoration work undertaken between 1963 and 1985 a museum housing some 500 exhibits was installed here. The Rococo, Classical, Romantic and Realist painting galleries are on the first floor of the former convent. The work of Josef Mánes – the central figure in 19th century Czech art – is surprisingly varied. The graceful painting *Josefina* is his most interesting work. The painters who decorated the National Theatre were dubbed as the 'National Theatre Generation'. Among them was Václav Brožík whose work *Hus at the Council in Constance* deserves special attention. Other artists represented here include Schikaneder, Pirner and Schwaiger, who prepared the way for Czech painting to move into the 20th century.

Daily (except Mon) 10.00-18.00 hrs; U milosr dných 1; Metro: Náměstí Republiky (B)

Bertramka –
Mozart museum **(C5)**
★ ☂ Between 1787 and 1791, Mozart was a frequent guest at the Dušeks' summer residence. It was at Bertramka that he composed the overture (292 inspired bars) to the opera *Don Giovanni* the night before the opera's hugely successful inaugural performance in what was then Nostic (now Stavovské) Theatre. It was also here that, three months

---

MARCO POLO SELECTION: MUSEUMS

1 Museum of Modern Art
Featuring a fascinating collection of 19th- and 20th-century French art (page 41)

2 Old Bohemian Art Collection
Gothic and Baroque masterpieces (page 45)

3 Bertramka
Mozart museum (page 40)

4 Smetana Museum
Homage to another great composer (page 44)

5 Technical Museum
Bugatti and Mercedes-Benz sports cars on show (page 43)

6 House at the Black Madonna
Exhibition of Cubism (page 41)

7 Jewish Museum
Major monument to Jewish culture (pqge 46)

8 Strahov Monastery
Library with ceiling frescos (page 45)

9 Decorative Arts Museum
Glass, porcelain and Cubist furniture (page 46)

10 Postage Museum
The *Penny Black*, the world's first stamp is kept here (page 44)

before his death, Mozart composed the aria *Io ti lascio, o cara, addio* for the diva Josefina Dušková. For the past 150 years, Bertramka has stood as a shrine to Wolfgang Amadeus Mozart, though the only physical vestiges of the great maestro exhibited in the house are 13 strands of his hair (the house as the composer knew it was ravaged by fire in 1871). Also on show are numerous letters, engravings, musical sketches, a grand piano, a two manual cembalo, and a clavichord on which Mozart played arias from *Don Giovanni*. There is a reconstruction of Mozart's bedroom which features a beautiful painting on the ceiling.

Daily 09.30-18.00 hrs; Mozartova; Metro: Anděl (B), then a 500 m walk

Bílkova vila –
Bílek Gallery (E2)

✝ You shouldn't miss the chance to visit this unusual house and explore the extravagant and expressive works of the Art Nouveau and Symbolist sculptor František Bílek (1872-1941). The architecture of the house, which was built to the artist's design in 1912, is based on (and decorated after) the concept of a field of grain, and it was intended to be a 'cathedral of art' as much as it was a family residence. Among the artist's well-known sculptures are *Spiritual Encounter* and *Future Conqueror*. Though unfortunately he remains little known elsewhere, Bílek's work was admired by many of his Czech contemporaries, and by Franz Kafka in particular.

15 May to 15 Oct daily (except Mon) 10.00-17.00 hrs; Mickiewiczova 1; Metro: Hradčanská (A)

Dům U černé Matky boží –
House at the Black Madonna (F3)

★ Architect Josef Gočár erected this beautiful Cubist building in 1911 on the site where a Baroque house had previously stood. The original 17th-century house sign of the Black Madonna has been integrated into the new façade. Inside is the Czech Museum of Fine Arts. The top two floors feature a permanent exhibition of Cubist art.

Daily (except Mon) 10.00-18.00 hrs; Celetná 34; Metro: Náměstí Republiky (B)

Dvořákovo muzeum –
Dvořák museum (F5)

This Museum dedicated to the great composer Antonín Dvořák (1841-1904) was opened in 1932. It is housed in the Baroque summer villa Amerika built between 1712 and 1720 by the renowned architect Kilian Ignaz Dientzenhofer. Dvořák was the artistic director of the New York Conservatory from 1892 to 1895 and was in the United States when he wrote his famous ninth *New World* symphony.

Daily (except Mon) 10.00-17.00 hrs; Ke Karlovu 20; Metro: I. P. Pavlova (C)

Galerie moderního umění –
Museum of Modern Art (G1)

★ This building is a masterpiece of the Czech functionalist movement, and was designed by Oldřich Tyl and Josef Fuchs and built between 1924 and 1928 for the Prague Trade Fair. Le Corbusier marvelled at the construction, which confirmed that his own nascent plans for the League of Nations palace in Geneva were indeed practicable. Following extensive renovations, the palace reopened in 1995 housing a museum of modern art. Among the highlights are selected works of 20th-century Czech art, as well as an interesting collection of 19th- and 20th-century French art and selected pieces of 20th-century European art. Particularly worth a mention are the Czech artists Mucha, Kdář, Šíma, Toyen, Kupka, Štýrský, Filla, Šimotová, the Janoušeks, Kolíbal and Gutfreund. The collection of French art is the most extensive outside France, Russia and the United States. A number of Impressionist paintings are exhibited here, including *In the Vegetable Garden* by Pissaro, *The Lovers* by Renoir, *Moulin Rouge* by Toulouse-Lautrec, *Bonjour, Monsieur Gauguin* by Gauguin and *The Green Cornfield* by Van Gogh. There is an impressive range of paintings by Sisley, Monet, Cézanne, Seurat, Rousseau and Matisse. (Rodin's sculptures *H. de Balzac*, *Meditation* and *John the Baptist* were first acquired and exhibited in Prague in 1902.) The exhibition also features 19 Picassos, dating mostly from the period between 1906 and 1913, which the art connoisseur V. Kramář bought from the then unknown artist – his 1907 self-portrait, for instance, commanded a price of 400 francs; its current value is estimated at several tens of millions of dollars. Braque, Chagall, Le Corbusier and Léger complete the collection. From the 20th-century European collection, Oskar Kokoschka stands out: his famous picture *The Red Egg* symbolizes the situation in Prague following the Munich treaty of 1938. The Norwegian artist Edvard Munch, who is represented here with his *Dance at the Seaside*, was particularly influential on Czech art after his Prague exhibition of 1905.

Daily (except Mon) 10.00-18.00 hrs; Letná, Dukelských Hrdinů 47; Metro: Vltavská (C), and trams 1 and 25

Historická expozice Národního muzea – Historical exhibition of the National Museum (D2)

Across from the Castle, the Lobkovic Palace houses a permanent exhibition on the development of Bohemia from prehistoric times to the present day. Amongst the oldest artefacts displayed are numerous Celtic finds. At one time, the Přemyslid kings had 60000 miners producing silver for coinage. An interesting collection of Renaissance jewellery (and noteworthy replicas of the Bohemian crown jewels), selected clocks and astrological instruments dating from the reign of Rudolf II (14th century) testify to the high quality of Czech craftsmanship in its heyday. There are also copies of the coronation seals, and an antique engraving depicting the execution of 27 Czech Protestant leaders that took place in 1621. An equally macabre sight is the sword allegedly used by the executioner, Mydlář. Numerous exhibits document the extent to which the French Revolution influenced the Czech national renaissance in the 19th century.

Daily (except Mon) 09.00-17.00 hrs; Metro: Hradčanská (A)

Kafka Museum (F3)

Since summer 1991, the Kafka Society has maintained a small

museum in a modern building on the site where the writer's family home once stood. Exhibitions render an impression of the author's life and work through photographs and quotations.

Daily (except Sun and Mon) 10.00-18.00 hrs; U radnice 5; Metro: Staroměstská (A)

Muzeum hlavního města Prahy – Prague Museum (H2)

The museum documents the history of Prague and the lives of its inhabitants. The main attraction is Antonín Langweil's model of the city, constructed between 1826 and 1837. The 20 sq m cardboard model shows the town centre as it stood in medieval times, before the 'sanitization' – particularly of the Jewish ghetto of Josefov – that took place in the second half of the 19th century. There is incredible detail in the Baroque decorated façades, windows, doors and sills, as well as the cobblestones. Today, it serves as a very useful reference for the architects of the town planning authority.

Daily (except Mon) 10.00-18.00 hrs; Karlín, Na poříčí 52; Metro: Florenc (B and C)

Národní technické muzeum – National Technical Museum (F1)

★ ♟ The exhibition space here covers 6000 sq m and serves to remind the many visitors who have forgotten that, until the Second World War, Czechoslovakia was among the world's foremost industrial nations. In the central hall stand the Prezident (1897), built in the Kopřivnice Factory (now Tatra) and the 12-cylinder Tatra (1935) which had a maximum speed of 140 km/h – quite

something for the time. Also worth exploring is the 600 m tunnel that runs under the museum, which is equipped with a mechanical model of an ore and coal mine.

Daily (except Mon) 09.00-17.00 hrs; Kostelní 42; Metro: Vltavská (C), trams 1 and 25

Národní galerie (Šternberský palác) – National Gallery (C2)

♟ Situated on the left behind the Archbishop's Palace on the Hradčanské náměstí is the Šternberk Palace, which houses the most important collection of old European art in Prague. Most strongly represented are Dutch, German and Italian artists. Of the Dutch pieces dating from the 14th to 16th centuries, the most notable are the *Madonna with St Luke* by Jan Gossaert, known as Mabuse, and the major landscape *Haymaking* by Pieter Breughel the Elder, which is shown alongside a series painted by Breughel the Younger. Two altar paintings by Peter Paul Rubens, a painting by Franz Hals and an early Rembrandt, *The Old Scholar*, are the highlights among the 17th-century Flemish pieces. There are works by German painters ranging from the 14th to 18th centuries; the most significant of these is the *Feast of the Rosary* by Albrecht Dürer, which was painted in 1506 in Venice and depicts the Virgin Mary with the Pope and the Holy Roman Emperor. Two altar paintings by Holbein the Elder, *Portrait of an Old Man* by Cranach the Elder and works by Albrecht Altdorfer are also displayed. In addition to the 14th- and 15th-century paintings, the 16th- to 18th-century

Italian collection (Tintoretto, Veronese) is worth seeing. Spanish art is represented by El Greco's *Head of Christ* and Goya's *Don Miguel Larzibadal*. There is also a fine collection of Russian icons. Though none of the artists featured in the 20th-century art collection are actually Czech-born, it includes impressive works by Gustav Klimt (*Virgins*) as well as Egon Schiele, Oskar Kokoschka and Edvard Munch. Take some time to linger in the French art section, which features paintings by all the usual masters from the Impressionist movement onwards (Monet, Cezanne, Van Gogh, Gauguin, Toulouse-Lautrec, Dufy and Matisse), plus some early Picassos and sculptures by Rodin. Picnics are permitted in the gardens.
Daily (except Mon) 10.00-18.00 hrs; Hradčanské náměstí 15; Metro: Hradčanská

Národní muzeum – National Museum (G4)

The monumental neo-Renaissance building that houses this museum – which is 104 m long, 76 m high and has a 70 m dome – was built by the Czech Josef Schulz in 1890, as a symbol of national rebirth. The allegorical figures on the parapet represent Bohemia; the Elbe is depicted as an old man, the Vltava as a virgin. The museum is organized in two separate sections, covering history and natural sciences. A tour of Europe's largest collection of minerals is highly recommended (an exceptional 40-carat diamond is one of the exhibit's highlights). There is an impressive collection of coins and medals dating back to the Přemyslid dynasty. The library contains one million volumes and 8000 manuscripts, including some priceless examples from the Middle Ages.
Daily 10.00-18.00 hrs; Wed 10.00-21.00 hrs; Václavské náměstí; Metro: Muzeum (A and C)

Poštovní muzeum – Postage Museum (G2)

★ Not even the staff dare estimate the number of stamps assembled here. The most valuable items on display include the world's first stamp, the *Penny Black* from England, the *Blue Mercury* stamp block and a collection of first stamps from all the countries of Europe.
Daily (except Mon) 09.00-16.30 hrs; Nové mlýny 2; Metro: Náměstí Republiky (B)

Smetana Museum (E3)

★ ⚓ ⚓ Not far from the Charles Bridge, on the banks of the Vltava, stands the Smetana Museum, named after Bedřich

Old field weapons: the Military Museum

Smetana (1824-94), the father of Czech nationalist music. It offers a panoramic view of the Castle and the Little Quarter. In the museum are letters, photographs, manuscripts of Smetana's compositions and some of his personal effects, such as the piano he played during his 5-year stay in Sweden. Tour the museum to strains of Smetana's *Moldau* (composed in 1874, when he had already gone deaf) accompanied by the soft sounds of the Vltava flowing past.

Scheduled to open in Autumn 1996; Novotného lávka; Metro: Staroměstská (A)

Staré české umění – Old Bohemian Art Collection (D2)

★ This gallery in St George's Monastery (973) features works from the 14th to 18th centuries, including some unique Gothic masterpieces. The basement holds the beautiful tympanum from St Mary of the Snows (1346), an equestrian portrait of St George (1373) and numerous Madonnas. A separate room displays the artistically magnificent but anonymous nine-part altarpiece showing scenes from the life of Christ. Another room is dedicated to panels (1357-67) by the artist Master Theodoric, whose talents were commissioned by the court of Charles IV. A further room is dominated by the votive painting of archbishop Jan Očko of Vlašim. On the ground floor are two tableaux with biblical themes (c. 1380) by Master Trebon, Bohemia's most important Gothic artist. Mannerist works from the court of Rudolf II and the Baroque period are shown on the first

floor. Works by Bartholomeus Spranger hang alongside portraits by Karel Škréta, and works by Petr Brandl, Jan Kupecký and Václav Vavřinec Reiner. Also represented are the masters of High Baroque – the sculptor Matthias Braun, his contemporary Ferdinand Maximilian Brokoff and Ignác Platzer.

Daily (except Mon) 10.00-18.00 hrs; Jiřský klášter; Metro: Hradčanská (A)

Strahovský klášter – Strahov Monastery (C3)

★ ☙ The monastery was founded in 1140 by Prince Vladislav II, making it the second oldest in Prague. It rapidly developed into the centre of intellectual life, serving as a seat of learning for the young Bohemian aristocracy. As the monastery was severely damaged by French bombardment in 1741, the present-day structure dates largely from the 17th and 18th centuries. Its library is one of the most celebrated sights in Prague. The Theological Hall, built on the first floor between 1671 and 1679 by Giovanni Domenico Orsi, is lined with Baroque bookcases holding theological literature – the display cabinets above the doors are for *libri prohibiti*. At the centre of the room are geographical and astrological globes. The frescos on the ceilings are the fruits of four years' labour by the monk Siardus Nosecký. One hundred years later, at the time of the French philosophical school known as the Encyclopaedists, the Philosophical Hall was built. It contains richly carved bookcases and ceiling frescos by Franz

Anton Maulpertsch, created in 1794. The Museum for Czech Literature surveys the development of national literature from the 9th century to the present day. A new exhibition of previously unseen Gothic works was inaugurated in 1994.

Daily (except Mon) 09.00-12.00 and 13.00-17.00 hrs; Strahovské nádvoří 132; Metro: Hradčanská (A)

Uměleckoprůmyslové muzeum – Decorative Arts Museum (E2)

★ This fantastic glass, porcelain and ceramic collection consists of more than 16 000 exhibits from antiquity to the present day. Particularly worth seeing are the worked gold articles, a collection of clocks and timepieces from around 1600 and the collection of Czech cubist furniture dating from 1910 to 1923.

Daily (except Mon) 10.00-18.00 hrs; Ul. 17 listopadu 2; Metro: Staroměstská (A)

Vojenské muzeum – Museum of Military History (C2)

This museum is situated near the Castle, inside one of Prague's most beautiful Renaissance structures. The façade of Schwarzenberg Palace features a geometric black and white sgraffito pattern in the Florentine style (1545-63). The exhibition within illustrates the evolution of the Czech army, from the Přemyslid principality to the declaration of the Czechoslovak republic at the end of the First World War. In the courtyard are some historic cannons and other artillery of Austro-Hungarian and Prussian provenance.

Daily May to Oct (except Monday), 10.00-18.00 hrs; Hradčanské náměstí 2; Metro: Hradčanská (A)

Židovské muzeum u Praze – Jewish Museum (E-F2)

★ ♘ By the 10th century, a community of Jewish merchants and traders were firmly settled in Prague. Their homes were clustered around what is now known as the Old-New Synagogue. Scientific and cultural life blossomed within the community, particularly during the 16th and 17th centuries. In the 19th century this ghetto became known as Josefov, named after the Emperor Joseph II, who exercised tolerance towards what was by this time a significant Jewish population. Then tragically, in 1893, the area was completely 'sanitized' and the Jews forced to move on. Only a few historically significant monuments were left standing. During the Second World War the Nazis, whose regime annihilated 90% of the city's Jewish population, brought to Prague numerous cultural and religious artefacts taken from 153 exterminated religious communities in Bohemia and Moravia, with the aim of creating a 'Museum of an extinct race'. In so doing, they unwittingly laid the foundation for the State Jewish Museum opened in 1950, that documents the culture and religion of the Jewish people. All that remains of the centre of old Prague are the cemeteries, synagogues, ceremonial hall and the Jewish Town Hall (which now houses a huge kosher restaurant) and the Old-New Synagogue (Staronová synagóga), the oldest synagogue in Europe still in use, and one of the oldest Gothic edifices in Prague. It is thought to have been built by Franciscan monks in

The library in the Strahov monastery

around 1280. The tympanum was chiselled from a single stone, and portrays a vine (the tree of life) with twelve roots symbolizing the twelve tribes of Israel. A large flag hangs from the vaulting. This was a gift from Ferdinand II in recognition of the bravery displayed by the Jews during the battle against the Swedes in 1648. The pulpit is divided by a Gothic wrought iron grille. Only men are allowed to pray in the main area; the galleries are reserved for women. During services, the honorary chair that once belonged to the revered Rabbi Löw remains unoccupied. The great Synagogue (or Jubilee Synagogue) is not in the former ghetto but in Jeruzalémská ulice (**G3**) and was built in 1906 in the Moorish style. In contrast to the Old-New synagogue, here the entire congregation is seated in the main hall during services. Since 1995, a festival of Jewish culture has been held here (May to October). The Baroque Klausen Synagogue (Klausova synagóga), (1694), contains the most complete exhibition of Judaica, including displays illustrating daily life, holidays, weddings, prayers, schools and traditional cooking. The walls of the 11th century Pinkas Synagogue (Pinkasova synagóga) are inscribed with the names of the 77 297 Czech Jews killed in concentration camps. It is currently under renovation. The Maisl synagogue (Maislova synagóga) was founded and financed by Mordechai Maisl, the wealthiest and most influential man in king Rudolph's Prague, in 1590-2. On the ground floor, an exhibit entitled 'The History of the Jews in Bohemia and Moravia' features religious objects, crowns, lamps, and goblets. The Ceremonial Hall (Obřadní sín) is part of the old Jewish cemetery. There is a moving display of images from the Terezín concentration camp, including children's drawings.

All buildings, daily (except Sat) 09.30-19.00 hrs, Old-New Synagogue 09.00-18.00 hrs; Maiselova; Tel: 2 31 03 02 for arranging guides and groups; Metro: Staroměstská (A)

Eat your heart out

Prague's famous wine restaurants – the Vinárna *– have been serving excellent wine and culinary specialities for centuries*

Just before sending him off to the guillotine, Robespierre reproached the gourmet Danton before the revolutionary tribunal with the assertion that his penchant for copious eating and drinking, Danton's renowned 'excesses', only served to compound his other offences. Likewise, when the country was in the grip of 'real socialism', visions of a rosy future were presented to the people, but the reality remained puritanical, grey and dreary. Czech culinary culture was repressed by the communist regime and it wasn't until the aftermath of the Velvet Revolution and the country's belated opening to tourism that gastronomic monotony and culinary stagnation were banished for good.

This explains why our knowledge of traditional Bohemian cuisine tends to be limited to dumplings and pickles. Our expectations are not high, and we can only be pleasantly surprised to discover that there is a real Czech cuisine, which is both substantial and flavourful.

In the better restaurants such as the Palace Hotel, painstakingly prepared dishes are created to meet the higher expectations of an international, elegant and cultivated clientele. The exclusive atmosphere and haute cuisine of 'Flambée' is lauded in gourmet circles, while steak lovers have a feast at 'U červeného kola'. At 'U Mecenáše', Mr Koubek delights in guiding customers through a gastronomic labyrinth. Numerous restaurants specialize in wild game: the chefs at 'Myslivana' and 'U Vladaře' have elevated pheasant, venison and wild boar (and even bear!) to please the most discriminating of palates. Good quality, good value cuisine may be found at 'Klášterní vinárna' and 'U tří housliček' while at Pelikan, guests may select any combination from ten menus.

Since the Velvet Revolution of 1989, most restaurants in Prague have become privately owned, and, as a consequence, culinary standards have risen. The political changes the country has under-

The locals gather under the shade of trees to enjoy a cool beer in a traditional beer garden

gone have spilled over into the gastronomic realm, and new eateries are springing up like mushrooms – and their names, opening times, menus and prices fluctuate with frustrating regularity. This growth spurt has been to the detriment of the traditional state-run (in other words, affordable) establishments, which are well on the way to becoming extinct. Still, other venues are rising to the challenge and putting up an excellent fight – good food and wine may be found at 'U čerta', 'U kamenného stolu' and 'U zlaté studně'. In the Czech Republic, restaurants and taverns can be divided into five price categories. First there are the expensive top class restaurants which are listed on page 56. The restaurants that fall into the first category are mainly five-star hotels and selected chic venues, while the majority of the good value finds fall into the second category. The third and fourth categories are mostly applied to taverns, inns (*hostinec*) and pubs (*pivnice*). As a general rule the pubs serve fine Czech beer, but it's difficult to find good or substantial food in them.

The typical Czech dining experience starts off with the popular aperitif *Becherovka*, a slightly bitter redcurrant liqueur from Karlovy Vary, which is served with ice, a lemon wedge and sometimes tonic. Another option is vodka, or the smooth *slivovice* (a quetsch *eau de vie* made in Jelínek). For the first course you can usually choose from a wide range of soups (*polévky*), such as the tasty *bramboračka* (potato and mushroom soup), or the selection of hors d'oeuvres (*předkrmy*). Some of the more exclusive restaurants serve real Russian caviar, which should be accompanied with ice-cold vodka. Often, the customer is presented with a trolley piled with hot and cold hors d'oeuvres to choose from.

When it comes to main courses, the selection is even more vast. Some classic choices include *svíčková na smetaně* (roast beef in a delicate bittersweet cream sauce with dumplings), *vepřová pečeně se zelím* (roast pork with cabbage) or *pečená husa* (roast goose). In addition to the usual potatoes and dumplings, new side dishes have begun to appear, such as *bramborák*, a kind of potato fritter with garlic and marjoram that is a perfect accompaniment for the wide array of meat dishes on offer. To satisfy the gourmet eye and palate, waiters will often flambé some of the main courses in vodka, gin or cognac at the table.

A *digestif* is a memorable experience, and not just for the stomach. Cognac is served in one of the 'Giant Snifters' from the celebrated Moser glass factory at Karlovy Vary. Depending on the physiognomy of the guest, the waiter selects an appropriate glass – they all have names such as Long Face, Moon Face, Long Fellow, Stout Gentleman, Slim Lady and Big Bertha! In restaurants such as 'U mecenáše', the waiter will put on a real show, juggling the filled glass over the flames which he then extinguishes with a magician-like flourish.

In Prague it is not customary to have cheese at the end of a meal, as the choices are limited and the quality inconsistent. Likewise, fresh salads are a rarity out of season. Desserts (*moučníky*), however, are another matter entirely – menus are filled with mouth-watering sweets such as *palačinky*, *lívanec*, *dort* and *buchta;* pastries stuffed with plums, raspberries or cherries and served with fromage blanc sprinkled with poppy seeds; caramel flambéd fruit and refined ice creams.

For many years, a war over who brews the best beer has been raging amongst Prague's 900 pubs. The real beer aficionados swear by the prestigious Pilsner Urquell or Pilsner Gambrinus (the 1993 beer of the year), Budvar, Radegast (the beer of 1994), Krušovice beer, Staropramen, Bráník or Pragovar. Westerners consider the first five of the series to be the best, although fans will argue long and loud in defence of the other contenders. Competition is constant between hundreds of pubs (specifically their landlords), over the most skilfully poured Pilsner Urquell. The freshest, smoothest Pilsner is poured at 'U zlatého tygra'. Another favourite is 'U kalicha', the walls of which are decorated with sayings and engravings recounting the story of the brave soldier Schwejk (it was here that he wanted to meet Sapper Vodička 'at six o'clock after the war').

When it comes to atmosphere and romance, the centuries-old taverns and stylish wine bars tucked away in the Baroque houses of the old town and Malá Strana have plenty of both. A number of these venues occupy vaulted Gothic cellars, on what six centuries ago was the ground floor. During the 17th century, the streets and squares were raised by one level in an effort to reduce the damage from flooding, so guests entering a 17th-century Baroque house need only descend a staircase to find themselves immersed in a 14th-century setting. Gothic and

---

MARCO POLO SELECTION: RESTAURANTS

1 Lobkovická vinárna
Lovely wine bar in the Little Quarter (page 57)

2 Myslivna
Game a speciality (page 58)

3 Parnas
Great food, lovely view (page 57)

4 Pelikán
Modern restaurant (page 58)

5 Klášterní vinárna
Solid, reliable restaurant (page 57)

6 Česká hospoda
Good value restaurant (page 61)

7 Gany's
Food for the calorie conscious (page 58)

8 U staré Synagogy
Good food in lovely Art Nouveau setting (page 58)

9 Red hot and blues
Tex-mex and jazz (page 57)

10 Valdštejnská
Rich menu in old-fashioned setting (page 60)

Romanesque ground floors have since become the cellars of popular establishments such as 'U pavouka', 'U kamenného stolu', 'U zlaté studně' and 'Flambée'.

Less intimate and more modern are the city's many snack bars and bistros, where *bufets* are comprised of a sandwich and a cheap glass of wine and the ubiquitous *automats* serve a wine 'du jour' to accompany very reasonably priced food. There are also a number of stands where at any time of day you can purchase a small pitcher of wine to wash down a hot sausage smothered in mustard. Tourists, who are generally surprised at this surfeit of choice, have recently dubbed Wenceslas Square 'the stomach of Prague'. Unlike the restaurants, which have recovered nicely from the hardships of the socialist regime, Prague's cafés (*kavárna*) remain relatively morose and anonymous – sometimes even downright shabby. It is hard to imagine that, during the period prior to the Second World War, these places were important cultural centres frequented by artists and journalists who would come to read local and foreign newspapers and chat over a cup of coffee. It was in the celebrated café Slavia that Smetana composed music, Rilke wrote poetry and the poet and Nobel prize winner Jaroslav Seifert drank coffee and rubbed shoulders with with the painter Toyen. During the 1920s, Kafka, Brod, Kisch and Werfel among others would gather regularly at the 'Arco' (*daily 11.00-02.00 hrs; Hybernská 16; Metro: Náměstí Republiky*). One of the few cafés that has managed to preserve its original Art Nouveau setting and the charms of a bygone era is the beautiful 'Evropa' café on Wenceslas Square.

Despite the current surge of interest in Prague and the influx of tourists, visitors will find that Prague is still a cheap place to eat and drink. Be advised, however, that it is worthwhile to book a table at least one day in advance; for the really good restaurants, you should telephone to reserve a table before you leave home.

The Ghost in the British Embassy

Prague has its fair share of ghost stories. In his *Stories of an Old Austrian*, Count Alfons Clary Aldringen told the eerie tale of the British Embassy ghost: 'When the Palais Thurn was sold to the British Embassy in 1920, Sir George and Lady Clark moved in. He was a diplomat of the old school while she was slightly 'bohemian' and artistically inclined. One day, I came across the couple looking very distraught. Apparently, the evening before, while the ambassador was talking to the chauffeur, Lady Clark had come flying down the stairs in terror screaming that she had seen a man in medieval clothing, carrying his head under his arm! On hearing of this incident, I informed them that a member of the Thurn family, who had previously occupied the house, had, in fact, been beheaded...'

CAFÉS

(T) = Terrace

Amadeus   (F3)
Eighty years ago, Einstein used to play violin on the first floor of the 'House with the Stone Table'. Today, the café Amadeus offers visitors to Prague a pleasant view of the Staroměstské náměstí.
Staroměstské náměstí 18; Metro: Můstek (A and B)

Bílý jelínek –
The White Hart (T)   (F3)
♣ This café is situated in a Baroque house behind the Old Town Hall, opposite the house where Franz Kafka was born. In fine weather, you can have coffee and cakes under the umbrellas on the terrace and watch the world go by.
Daily 10.00-24.00 hrs; U radnice 12-14; Metro: Staroměstská (A)

Café-Bar (T)   (F3)
In the Renaissance house on the Staroměstské náměstí, fine sgraffito portrays scenes from ancient mythology. Franz Kafka spent much of his childhood here. 30 different kinds of tea and coffee.
Daily 10.00-23.00 hrs; Staroměstské náměstí 3/2; Metro: Staroměstská (A)

The terrace cafés of the Old Town

Café-Poet (T) (D2)

Comfortable café and restaurant situated to the left of the main entrance to Prague Castle.

Daily 09.00-20.00 hrs; Metro: Hradčanská (A)

Espresso U Dominikána (F3)

In the town centre, six varieties of coffee, Irish coffee, wine, cold and hot food, good desserts.

Daily 10.00-22.00 hrs; Husova 4; Metro: Národní třída (B)

Euroclub (G4)

Café and restaurant. Wines from southern Moravia, exhibitions and jazz concerts.

Daily 10.00-23.00 hrs; Opletalova 5; Metro: Muzeum (A and C)

Evropa (T) (G4)

A treat for lovers of Art Nouveau. Original lamps and chandeliers, murals and mirrors decorate the interior. The lovely horseshoe balcony has been reopened. Live music.

Wed to Sun 15.00-24.00 hrs; Václavské náměstí 29; Metro: Můstek (A and B)

Gany's (F4)

Thirties Art Deco café with seven billiard tables in two rooms. English and German papers, Radegast beer, several kinds of coffee, breakfast c. 50 Kč.

Daily 08.00-23.00 hrs; Národní 20; Metro: Národní třída (B)

Kajetánka (T) (D2)

☙ Directly beneath the castle approach, located in the former Church of St Mary. The café has a terrace with a great view of the Little Quarter, Strahov monastery and the New Town.

Daily 11.00-20.00 hrs; in the winter 11.00-18.00 hrs; Kajetánské zahrady; Metro: Hradčanská (A)

Milena (F3)

This venue is named after one of Kafka's lovers, Milena Jesenská (*Letter to Milena*). The café is housed in the Franz Kafka Society building, opposite the Old Town Hall, and was designed as a 1920s-style café. Great live piano music.

Daily 10.00-22.00 hrs; Staroměstské náměstí 22; Metro: Staroměstská (A)

Palace (F3)

A modern café within a lovely Art Nouveau hotel (1906) in the centre of town, opposite the main Post Office. This is where Franz Kafka staged the only public readings of his own work. Several varieties of coffee. Expensive.

Daily 06.00-01.00 hrs; Panská 12; Metro: Můstek (A and B)

Paříz (F3)

Situated in a Neo-Gothic building (1904) featuring fine examples of Art Nouveau, this pleasant café has a wide selection of coffees and cakes.

Daily 06.30-01.00 hrs; U obecního domu 1; Metro: Náměstí Republiky (B)

Ponton (E3)

☙ This elegant venue serves nothing but Champagne and sparkling wines, and has an excellent, unusual view of the Charles Bridge and the Castle (open only between Easter and October).

Daily 11.00-24.00 hrs; Alšovo nábřeží; Metro: Staroměstská (A)

Slavia (E4)

☙ ☯ This historic café (1863) just opposite the National The-

Historical spot: artists and poets have been meeting here for over a century

atre was a meeting place for musicians such as Bedřich Smetana, writers like Karel Čapek and Nobel prize winner Jaroslav Seifert. From the large window looking over the Vltava and Hradčany, Rainer Maria Rilke composed his poetic declaration of love to Czech Prague, *Larenopfer*.
Národní 1; Metro: Národní třída (B)

U bakaláře (F3)
A student café in the city centre, with cheap food and drink. Also a good place for breakfast.
Mon-Fri 08.30-19.00 hrs, Sat/Sun 13.00-19.00 hrs; Celetná 13; Metro: Náměstí Republiky (B)

U mostecké věže (D3)
By the bridge tower, on the site occupied by the Swedes during the siege of the Little Quarter in 1648. Today, the same spot is invaded by tourists of every nationality. Snacks, beer, wine and coffee.
Daily 10.00-24.00; Mostecká 3; Metro: Malostranská (A)

U Týna (T) (F3)
Beneath the Gothic arch in front of the Týn Church. From the terrace, you can hear the bells of the astronomical clock chiming the hour. A good place to enjoy a glass of wine.
Daily 10.00-22.00 hrs; Staroměstské náměstí 15; Metro: Můstek (A and B)

Velryba (E4)
🚶 This simple and reasonably priced café is located in the centre of Prague, and is popular with students.
Daily 11.00-02.00 hrs; Opatovická 24; Metro: Národní (B)

RESTAURANTS

Category 1
Meal for one person including wine, 600-1000 Kč

Čertovka (T) (E3)
〰️ Tucked away on the banks of the river – you can gain access to this restaurant via a narrow staircase. Nice view of the Old Town.

The Gourmet Palaces of Prague

Club Restaurant (F3)

The Hotel Palace offers Bohemian and international cuisine in a restaurant with a combination of Art Nouveau and Art Deco styles. *From 1000 Kč.Daily 19.00-01.00 hrs; Panská 12; Tel 24 09 31 11; Metro: Můstek (A and B)*

Flambée (F3)

Romanesque and Gothic cellar steeped in history. A special favourite is the 'Perch en papillote'. From 800 Kč . *Daily 11.30-01.00 hrs; Husova 5; Tel: 24 24 85 12; Metro: Národní (B)*

Gourmet (Villa Voyta) (O)

Although situated on the edge of town, you will need to book a table at least two days in advance. Wonderful game dishes, such as duck or venison steaks, served with wines from north Bohemia. From 700 Kč. *Daily 12.00-24.00 hrs; K. novému dvoru 124/54; Tel: 4 72 55 11; Praha 4; Metro: Kačerov (C)*

Opera Grill (E3)

In a small stylish room that seats no more than 24 people, you can settle into a comfortable armchair and chat with the young proprietor. An aura of luxury permeates as you eat with silver cutlery among porcelain statues and original paintings. The chef is proud of his duck with *bramborák*. Good Zernoseky white wines, and red from Roudnice. From 900 Kč. *Daily 19.00-02.00 hrs; Karoliny Světlé 35; Tel: 26 55 08; Metro: Staroměstská (A)*

U mecennáše (D3)

This restaurant still ranks as one of Prague's best. In the first room is the executioner's table, dating from 1634; the second room is where all the VIPs sit. Top quality Bohemian cuisine, good wines, and friendly service from Mr Koubek. From 600 Kč. *Daily 17.00-24.00 hrs; Malostranské náměstí 10; Tel: 53 38 81; Metro: Malostranská (A)*

U pavouka (F3)

Enter this 17th-century Baroque house, descend the 32 steps and you will find yourself transported to the Gothic age. A bricked-up Gothic window in the cellar once gave directly on to the street. The atmosphere is intimate and food is of a consistently high standard. Try the 'Chicken Bombay'. From 700 Kč. *Daily 12.00-24.00 hrs; Celetná 17; Tel: 24 81 14 36; Metro: Můstek (A and B)*

U zlaté hrušky (C2)

This luxury restaurant stands in the picturesque lane, Nový svět. The interior is stylish, the atmosphere homely and the delicacies exquisite. You can also dine in the beautiful gardens. Lunch from 300 Kč, Dinner from 1000 Kč. *Daily 11.30-15.00 hrs and 18.30-24.00 hrs; Nový svět 3; Tel. and Fax: 53 11 33; Metro: Hradčanská (A)*

Daily 11.00-23.00 hrs; Tel: 53 88 53; U lužického semináře 24; Metro: Malostranská (A)

David (D3)

Near the US embassy. Good cooking, good wines and a pleasant atmosphere.

Daily 12.00-15.00 hrs and 18.30-23.30 hrs; Tržiště 21; Tel: 53 93 25; Metro: Malostranská (A)

Halali Restaurant (F3)

Specialities include Hungarian dishes and game such as wild boar, venison, hare and turkey, accompanied by lively Romany music.

Daily 18.00-02.00 hrs; Václavské náměstí 5-7; Tel: 24 19 36 89; Metro: Můstek (A and B)

John Bull (G3)

English restaurant serving Czech and English dishes and beers.

Daily 11.00-23.00 hrs, Fri 19.00-21.00 Jazz; Senovážná 8; Tel: 24 22 60 05; Metro: Náměstí Republiky (B)

Kampa club (T) (E3)

Situated in the quiet Kampa square, specializing in both Bohemian and international dishes; game is a particular speciality here.

Daily 12.00-15.00 hrs and 18.00-24.00 hrs; Na Kampě 14; Tel: 53 06 36; Metro: Malostranská (A)

Klášterní vinárna (E4)

★ Great cooking and a comfortable atmosphere can be found in this former convent, which serves what is arguably the best pepper steak in Prague.

Daily 11.30-15.30 hrs and 17.30-24.00 hrs; Národní třída 8; Tel: 29 05 96; Metro: Národní třída (B)

Lobkovická vinárna (D3)

★ Stylish and in keeping with the aristocratic tastes of the Little Quarter, this restaurant stands next to the German embassy. It was built 100 years ago by Prince Lobkovic. Good steaks.

Daily 12.00-15.00 hrs and 18.30-24.00 hrs; Vlašská 17; Tel: 53 01 85; Metro: Malostranská (A)

Molly Mallone's (F3)

Irish pub. Irish, English and Czech beer and steaks.

Daily 12.00-01.00 hrs; U obecního dvora 4; Tel: 23 16 222; Metro: Náměstí Republiky (B)

Nebozízek (T) (D4)

◁▷ Reached by cable car, this restaurant is perched on Petřín Hill, 100 m above the Vltava, and offers food that rivals the spectacular view.

Daily 11.00-18.00 hrs and 19.00 -23.00 hrs; Petřínské sady; Tel: 53 79 05, Fax: 55 10 17; Metro: Národní třída (B)

Parnas (E4)

★ ◁▷ Fantastic view over Hradčany and the Charles Bridge. This is the ideal place to indulge in delicate Norwegian fish specialities and good international cuisine while looking out over the river. The interior is decorated with marquetry, green marble and a beautiful long bar. French and Californian wine. Brunch on Sundays with jazz. (11.00-15.00 hrs).

Daily 12.00-15.00 hrs and 18.30-23.00 hrs; Smetanovo nábřeží 2; Tel: 24 22 76 14; Metro: Národní třída (B)

Red Hot and Blues (F3)

★ American restaurant serving up Texan specialities. Jazz nights.

Daily 09.00-23.00 hrs, jazz on Wed, Fri, Sat, brunch in the garden on Sat and Sun; Jakubská 12; Tel: 23 14 639; Metro: Náměstí Republiky (B)

U staré synagogy
(The Old Synagogue) (C2)

★ Near the Old Synagogue. The menu of this luxury restaurant includes old Bohemian specialities. Pleasant Art Nouveau interior with live piano music.

Daily 11.30-24.00 hrs; Pařižká 17; Tel: 2 31 85 52; Metro: Staroměstská (A)

U Vladaře (D3)

Old Prague dishes and game served in a genuine olden-day setting. Good wines. Menus priced from 350-600 Kč.

Daily 11.00-01.00 hrs; Maltézské náměstí 10; Tel: 53 81 28; Metro: Malostranská (A)

Category 2

Meal for one person including wine, from 300 Kč

Gany's (F4)

★ Cuisine for the calorie conscious, with a choice of four salads all the year round (which is still something of a rarity in Prague). Vegetarian meals, fish, chicken. Reasonable prices.

Daily 11.00-23.00 hrs; Národní 20, 1st floor; Tel: 29 76 65; Metro: Národní třída (B)

Košer restaurace (E2)

Situated in the Jewish Town Hall. 540 crowns buys you a good five-course meal served in a simple setting.

Sun-Thurs 12.00-20.00 hrs, Fri 12.00-16.00, Sat 12.00-13.30 hrs; Maislova 18; Tel: 24 81 09 29; Metro: Staroměstská (A)

Letenský zámeček (F1)

Opposite the Technical Museum is the second oldest carousel in the world. A few steps further on are the three restaurants of the Letenský zámeček. The garden restaurant offers traditional Bohemian cuisine and good Kozel beer at reasonable prices. The prices and food in the restaurant 'Ullmann' are similar, while next door in the restaurant 'Belcredi' a good meal costs 200-400 Kč. You can have coffee or a cognac in the small room in the castle tower, and enjoy a fine view.

Ullmann, daily 10.00-24.00 hrs; Tel: 37 12 06; Belcredi, daily 11.00-02.00 hrs; Metro: Vltavská (C) and trams 1 and 25 (2nd stop)

Monica (F4)

Quiet restaurant serving good food, whether fish, steaks, vegetarian or desserts. Prices range from 50-280 Kč.

Daily 12.00-24.00 hrs; Charvátova; Tel: 24 21 20 31; Metro: Národní třída (B)

Myslivna (I4)

★ Pheasant – 'food for the gods' according to Voltaire – wild duck, and other game served with *bramborák* potatoes.

Daily 12.00-16.00 hrs and 17.00-24.00 hrs; Jagelonská 21; Tel: 6 27 02 09; Metro: Flora (A)

Pelikán (F3)

★ Good food, excellent service, decent prices. The glass wall provides the perfect opportunity for people-watching as passers-by meander through the pedestrian precinct. Bohemian cuisine.

Daily 11.30-16.00 hrs and 18.00-23.00 hrs; Na příkopě 7; Tel: 24 21 06 97; Metro: Můstek (A and B)

Golden Fountain - U zlaté studně

(D2) High above the rooftops of the Little Quarter – which has finally been renovated – just beneath the Castle, stands the traditional terrace restaurant. After dark, the legendary hundred towers of Prague, the moon and the stars, all seem within reach from here. The calm pervading this spot even affected the German and Czech students who, back in the days of increasing nationalism, would sit here peacefully taking turns to sing their anthems, Wacht am Rhein and Hej Slované.

U Golema (E2)

Immerse yourself in the atmosphere of this magical place where the *Golem* once caused havoc. A gilded sculpture of the mythical figure, created by Rabbi Löw, stands in the largest room. Try the 'Rabbi's Bag' (*rabínova kapsa*).

Daily Mon-Fri 11.00-22.00 hrs, Sat 17.00-23.00 hrs, Closed Sun; Maiselova 8; Tel: 2 32 81 65; Metro: Staroměstská (A)

U kamenného stolu (F3)

It was in the first floor rooms of this establishment, formerly the salon of Madame Fanta, that Einstein first presented his Theory of Relativity to a spellbound audience that included Max Brod and Franz Kafka in 1910. Two restaurants; good Moravian wine.

Daily 11.00-14.00 hrs and 18.00-23.00 hrs; Staroměstské náměstí 18; Tel: 24 21 20 26; Metro: Můstek (A and B)

U Lorety (T) (C3)

✝ This elegant restaurant complete with terrace stands opposite the Černín Palace. The menu features both Bohemian and international cuisine.

Daily 11.30-15.00 hrs and 18.00-23.00 hrs; Loretánské náměstí 8; Tel: 24 51 01 91; Metro: Hradčanská (A)

U pastýřky (G6)

Log cabin interior and traditional music, with good char-grilled meals and wine from the barrel. Reservations recommended.

Daily 18.00-01.00 hrs; Bělehradská 14; Tel. and Fax: 43 43 19; Metro: I. P. Pavlova (C) and trams 11 and 6

U Plebána (E3)

❖ Comfortable restaurant, serving international cuisine and traditional Czech specialities. Reservations are necessary in the evening.

Daily 12.00-24.00 hrs; Betlémské náměstí 10; Tel: 24 22 90 23; Metro: Národní třída (B)

U sv Jana Nepomuckého (C2)

Communion wine from the archbishop's cellars in South Moravia (which also supply the Vatican). Try the shrimps in cheese pastry.

Daily 09.00-22.00 hrs; Hradčanské nám. 12; Tel: 53 56 12; Metro: Hradčanská (A)

U zlaté studně (T) (D2)

Enjoy the panorama over the city rooftops from the enchanting wine bar terrace, on the 5th floor of the hotel. Re-opening Sept 1996 (at time of press).

U zlaté studně 166; Metro: Malostranská (A)

U zlaté podkovy (D3)

Pricewise, this restaurant does not belong in this category, but its setting, in an old-fashioned house in Neruda, and the interior are first-class. The sign shows St Wenceslas' horse with a golden horseshoe, after which it has been named. Traditional goulash, ribs and beer, reasonable prices for the area.
Daily 10.00-24.00 hrs; Nerudova 34; Metro: Malostranská (A)

Valdštejnská hospoda (D2)

★ Game, fish, beef and pork dishes on a rich menu in this fine old restaurant. The story of the 'Secret of the Fountain' is told on the plates. Reservations always necessary.
Daily 11.30-16.00 hrs and 18.00-23.00 hrs; Valdštejnské nám. 7; Tel: 53 87 04; Metro: Malostranská (A)

Vikárka (D2)

It was 430 years ago that the vicar received permission from the archbishop to serve wine to passing 'mortals'. Gothic cellar.
Daily 11.00-22.00 hrs; Vikářská 6; Tel: 24 51 06 86; Metro: Hradčanská (A)

Znojemská vinárna (F3)

An elegant restaurant serving South Moravian specialities such as Vranov schnitzel. Round off your meal with pancakes and Moravian wine.
Daily 11.30-23.00 hrs; Václavské náměstí 7; Tel: 24 19 36 90; Metro: Můstek (A and B)

Category 3

Meal for one person including wine or beer, from 100 Kč

Česká hospoda (G4)

★ Comfortable and clean restaurant, friendly service, good Bohemian cooking and fantastic beer. Crispy duck costs 86 Kč, Wienerschnitzel 75 Kč. 100 m from Wenceslas Square.
Daily 10.00-23.00 hrs; Krakovská 20; Tel: 261537; Metro: Muzeum (A and C)

Evropa (G4)

⚐ The Pilsner restaurant in the basement of the hotel. Evropa

Wine and coffee by the hourly chimes of the Loreta church

is decorated in beautiful Art Nouveau style. The atmosphere is better than the actual cooking. Try the pork with celery, onions and mushrooms (*vlatavský kari rendlik*). They serve good Pilsner on draught.

Daily 11.30-23.00 hrs; Václavské náměstí 29; Tel: 24 22 45 17; Metro: Můstek (A and B)

Jo's Bar (D3)

Canadian restaurant, Mexican food, Czech beer.

Daily 11.00-02.00 hrs; Malostranské náměstí 7; Tel: 531251; Metro: Malostranská (A), tram 12, 22.

Klub novinářů (F2)

A favourite watering hole for journalists and members of the press. The schnitzel in cheese sauce goes down well with a cool glass of Pilsner Urquell. Pleasingly low prices.

Daily 11.00-22.00 hrs; Pařižská 9; Tel: 2 32 26 18; Metro: Staroměstská (A)

Makarská (D3)

Fish, game, chicken and Bohemian dishes in the heart of the Little Quarter, served in a bar that is over a century old. Steak for 200 Kč. The bar serves good South Moravian and French wines.

Daily 12.00-24.00 hrs; closed Jan-Feb; Malostranské náměstí 2; Tel: 53 13 18; Metro: Malostranská (A)

Malostranská beseda (T) (D3)

The food served in this Renaissance house, formerly the town hall of the Little Quarter, is basic but very good.

Daily 11.00-23.00 hrs; Malostranské náměstí 21; Tel: 53 85 68; Metro: Malostranská (A)

Pálava (H4)

Traditional restaurant offering regional specialities. Delicious Moravian dishes and wines from Pavlovice in South Moravia.

Daily 11.00-23.00 hrs; Slavíkova 18; Tel: 6 27 52 73; Metro: Jiřího z Poděbrad (A)

Rostov (F3)

On the 6th floor, this quality modern restaurant offers good food and fine views.

Daily 11.00-23.00 hrs; Disco 21.00-04.00 hrs; Václavské náměstí 21; Tel. and Fax: 26 80 81; Metro: Můstek (A and B)

Tři grácie (T) (E3)

South Moravian specialities and wines from Mikulov. A stone's throw away from the historic Charles Bridge. Great view of the bridge from the terrace. Reservations are necessary during the peak season.

Daily 10.00-24.00 hrs; Novotného lávka 5; Tel: 24 22 91 06; Metro: Staroměstská (A)

U čerta (D3)

This small wine bar offers good food and excellent wines. Connoisseurs will particularly appreciate the Veltliner and Vinoteka wines. Reservations necessary in the evening.

Daily 11.30-23.00 hrs; Nerudova 4; Tel: 53 09 75; Metro: Malostranská (A)

U Fleků (T) (E4)

The most famous bar in town has become a popular meeting place for tourists. Lager has been lovingly brewed here for 500 years, while the 13% proof dark beer, with its characteristic smoky caramel aftertaste

Brewery and restaurant combined: a rendezvous for beer lovers from all over the world

has been brewed here since 1843. Seats 900 people.

Daily 09.00-23.00 hrs (Brass band music in the summer); Křemencova 11; Tel: 24 91 51 18; Fax: 29 68 79; Metro: Národní třída (B), then a 600-m walk (behind the National Theatre)

U kalicha (G5)

♜ This beer restaurant is a well-known tourist attraction. Bohemian cuisine, Pilsner beer on draught. Reservations required.

Daily 11.00-23.00 hrs; Brass band from 19.30; Na bojišti 12-14; Tel: 29 07 01, Fax: 29 19 45; Metro: I. P. Pavlova (C)

U krále brabantského (D2)

Under the new castle steps in the Little Quarter. A plaque mounted on the façade proclaims that around 600 years ago 'King Václav IV was often a guest here'. Good Moravian dishes and wines.

Daily 11.00-23.00 hrs; Thunovská 15; Tel: 5 61 81 98; Metro: Malostranská (A)

U malého Glena (D3)

American restaurant serving breakfast, lunch and dinner which is accompanied by live jazz every night (as well as reggae and acid jazz).

Daily 09.00-03.00 hrs; Karmelitská 23; Tel: 53 58 115; Metro: Malostranská (A), trams 12 and 22.

U Pešků (G5)

Good Bohemian cuisine and Pilsner Urquell. Reasonably priced, rarely overcrowded.

Daily 10.30-23.00 hrs, Sat and Sun 10.30-15.00 hrs; Sokolská 52; Tel: 29 19 30; Metro: I. P. Pavlova (C)

U Rudolfa (E2)

✵ The smallest wine bar in Prague in the heart of the Jewish Old Town. Good food – try their 'Rabbi's Bag'.

Daily 10.00-22.00 hrs; Maiselova 5; Tel: 2 32 26 71; Metro: Staroměstská (A)

U Schnellů (D3)

In the middle of the aristocratic Little Quarter, this famous restaurant (founded 1784) has served such illustrious clients as Peter the Great, and Saxon and Bavarian kings. Good Bohemian cooking.

Daily 11.00-24.00 hrs; Tomášská 2; Tel: 53 20 04; Metro: Malostranská (A)

U supa (F3)

During the Middle Ages, many restaurants lined Celetná, which is the ancient passageway between the Old Town Market (Staroměstské náměstí) and the Powder Tower. This is one of the survivors, offering Bohemian food and Pilsner Urquell.

Daily 11.30-23.00 hrs; Celetná 22;

Tel: 24 21 20 04; Metro: Můstek (A and B)

U tří housliček –
The Three Violins (D3)
Between 1667 and 1748, this building was occupied by three violin-making families, and legend has it that the chef played the violin while cooking to make the meat more tender.
Daily 11.00-24.00 hrs; Nerudova 12; Tel. and Fax: 53 47 21; Metro: Malostranská (A)

PUBS

Charlie-Pub (D3)
Completely new pub in the Little Quarter, located in an old Baroque house that features lovely frescos and arches. Pilsner Urquell and Domažlice beer make the ideal accompaniment to *Utopenec* and other good Bohemian dishes.
Daily 11.00-24.00 hrs; Míšeňská 10

Krušovická pivnice (F2)
Named after the beer it has on tap (Krušovice), which is served with reasonably priced food.
Daily 11.00-24.00 hrs; Široká 20

Skořepka (F3)
Gambrinus (voted Beer of the Year in 1993) as well as Purkmistr and Eisbein beers.
Daily (except Sun) 11.30-23.00 hrs; Skořepka 1

U Bubeníčků (E4)
A good place to sample the renowned Gambrinus beer from Plzeňand, accompanied by hard-to-beat traditional Bohemian cooking.
Daily 09.00-22.00 hrs, Sat and Sun 11.00-21.00 hrs; Myslíkova 6

U Černého vola (C3)
'The Black Cow' serves good Popovice beer on draught.
Daily 10.00-22.00 hrs; Loretánská náměstí 2

U dvou koček (F3)
'The Two Cats' features Pilsner Urquell alongside a number of other surprising brews. Traditional Bohemian food.
Daily 08.30-15.00 hrs and 16.00-23.00 hrs; Uhelný trh 10

U kocoura (D3)
'The Tomcat' serves Pilsner Urquell.
Daily 11.00-23.00 hrs; Nerudova 2

U Pinkasů (F3)
Good pils and Bohemian food for 60-160 Kč, in a house that was founded in 1843.
Daily 09.00-23.00 hrs; Jungmannova nám. 15

U svatého Tomáše (E2)
Named after St Thomas, this brewery was founded by the Augustines in 1358. Comfortable and relaxed, both inside and in the garden, where there is a summer barbecue. 8 varieties of beer. Brass band during the summer (20.00-24.00 hrs).
Daily 11.30-24.00 hrs; Letenská ulice 12

U Vejvodů (F3)
Staropramen beer. A good Bohemian menu, which is also good value.
Daily 10.00-23.00 hrs; Jilská 4

U zlatého tygra (F3)
Pilsner Urquell. The best beer in Prague. Presidents Clinton and Havel came here in 1994.
Daily 15.00-22.30 hrs; Husova 16

A shopper's paradise

On the Golden Cross, you can buy Bohemian glass and dark-red garnets, chic fashions, antiques and traditional crafts

With the exchange rate at around 40 Kč to the pound sterling, and 25 Kč to the dollar (August 1996 rates), there is good value shopping to be found in Prague. The most important shopping centre is the so-called Golden Cross, an elegant pedestrian precinct around Wenceslas Square, Na příkopě, ulice 28 října and Národní třída. This is a great place for buying glass, jewellery made from dark-red Bohemian granite, antiques, modern tapestry, objets d'art, LPs and CDs of classical music, as well as coffee-table books in various languages, and sundry souvenirs of Prague. Fashionable clothes, elegant hats, handbags and cheap leather goods can also be found. Shopping is made easier by the fact that many shopkeepers speak foreign languages, or at least are prepared to communicate with hand signals! Many places sell chic hats by Czech designers, and design collec-

Popular souvenirs: Bohemian glass

tions are available at Rytířská 22, Národní 23, suits at Panská 9. The extreme diversity on show in the windows of the many antique shops are a real feast for the eyes – you can find excellent glass and filigree work. A visit to the Moser Glass Company ('The Glass of Kings, The King of Glass') is well worth the time – if only to admire its wooden walls with fine marquetry and the valuable, hundred-year-old glass windows. In the better hotels there are also small shops with glass, porcelain and souvenirs. A novelty in Prague is the number of small private shops selling pictures, jewellery and miniatures of the city's most famous sights. Most prized by visitors are the Onion pattern from Dubí and Pirkenhammer porcelain from Karlovy Vary and Březová, as well as pictures, small sculptures and drawings by contemporary Prague artists, which can be found in the Platýz and Golden Lane galleries. For children, there are finely worked wooden toys – cars, trains, dolls and dolls' houses, and puppets.

An increasing number of shops and small businesses as well as restaurants now accept credit cards.

ANTIQUES

The antique shops in Prague are always worth a browse. Good clocks, porcelain, old pictures and small items of furniture can be found at Karmelitská 12, Na můstku 3, Václavské náměstí 17, and at ★ Athena's Treasury opposite the Old Jewish Cemetery.

ARTS & CRAFTS

Hand-woven textiles, handkerchiefs, puppets, ceramics and wood carvings are reasonably priced at the following places:

Lidová jizba (F4)
Václavské náměstí 14; Metro: Můstek (A and B)

Krásná jizba (F4)
★ *Národní třída 36; Metro: Národní třída (B)*

ART GALLERIES

The commercial art galleries that have sprung up in recent years are flourishing, but can be quite expensive.

Galerie Jiří Švestka (F4)
Christo and Warhol.
Jungmannova 30; Metro: Národní třída (B)

Galerie Pyramida (E4)
Signed ornamental glass.
Národní 11; Metro: Národní třída (B)

Golden Lane (D2)
Hradčany; Metro: Hradčanská (A)

Platýz (F3)
★ *Národní třída 37; Metro: Národní třída (B)*

MARCO POLO SELECTION: SHOPPING

1 Celetná ulice
Old books, prints, engravings and drawings (page 67)

2 Dlouhá třída
Granat – Bohemian granite (page 69)

3 Rytířská
Women's fashions (page 68)

4 Na příkopě
Moser – world-famous glassware (page 68)

5 Národní třída
Pbťyz – pictures by well-known artists (page 66)

6 Národní trída
Krásná jizba – traditional Czech arts and crafts (page 66)

7 Pařížská třída
Dior - cosmetic advice and treatment (page 67)

8 Staroměstské náměstí
Vlasta – excellent lace (page 69)

9 Jungmannova
All good Supraphon brand records and CDs (page 69)

10 U starého hřbitova
Athena's junk shop (page 66)

Staronová Galerie **(F2)**
Maiselova 15; Metro: Staroměstská
(A)

Zlatá lilie **(F3)**
Malé náměstí 12; Metro: Staroměstská
(A)

BOOKS

Books in all languages are available at Na příkopě 3, 27, and 31 and at Melantrich (corner of Wenceslas Square and Můstek). In Celetná 34, there is a wide selection of travel and art books. Foreign language art books can be found in Odeon and Melantrich. Check out the Lyra Pragensis collection of small illustrated, leather-bound books (priced at about 30 Kč each) – they make lovely gifts. On Thursdays bookshops are traditionally crowded, as that is the day new titles are released.

BOOKS (SECOND-HAND)

Though prices have recently gone up, you can still find some real treasures in Prague. Look out for old prints, engravings and books. At ★ Celetná 31, Křenek's by the Powder Tower, there are old German books, prints and engravings. At Karlova 2 there is a shop specializing in Art books and old drawings.

COINS

Numismatists will delight in the old medals and antique coins at Pařížská 8.

COSMETICS

The Institute For Medical Cos-

metics has been around for more that 30 years. Upon your arrival you will be examined by a dermatologist. Following your consultation, you will be placed in the hands of a qualified and experienced beautician who then administers the treatments using cosmetics produced in the Institute itself. Services are also available from staff psychiatrists, psychologists, gynaecologists and doctors specializing in weight problems. Plastic surgery can be performed here.

Christian Dior **(F2)**
★ Luxury cosmetics and treatments.
Pařížská 7; Metro: Staroměstská (A)
and *Národní 17; Metro: Národní*
třída (B)

Niňa Ricci **(F2)**
Pařižská 4; Metro: Staroměstská (A)

Ústav kosmetiky - Institute for Medical Cosmetics **(F4)**
Jungmannova ulice 31; Metro: Můstek
(A and B); Tel: 24 49 41 00

DEPARTMENT STORES

These shops are the places to purchase everyday items. Some of the larger stores have more or less become specialized: for children, try heading for Dětský Dům, Na příkopě 15; for fashionable clothing, take a look at Dům módy, Václavské náměstí 58.

Bílá labuť **(G2)**
Na poříčí 23;
Metro: Florenc (B and C)

Krone **(F3-4)**
Václavské náměstí 21;
Metro: Můstek (A and B)

Kotva (F3)
Náměstí republiky 8;
Metro: Náměstí republiky (B)

K-Mart (F4)
Národní třída 26;
Metro: Národní třída (B)

FASHION

This is an area where Prague has definitely made a lot of progress since the 'Velvet Revolution'. Young fashions and quality fabrics are widely available, which local tailors can transform into elegant outfits.

Adam (F3)
Celebrated gentlemen's tailor.
Na příkopě 8;
Metro: Můstek (A and B)

Aristone (F3)
U Prašné brány 3;
Metro: Náměstí Republiky (B)

Gianni Versace (F3)
U Prašné brány 3;
Metro: Náměstí Republiky (B)

Hugo Boss (F3)
Jungmannovo náměstí 18;
Metro: Můstek (A and B)

Pasáž u divadla (F3)
★ For everything a woman could possibly want.
Rytířská 22;
Metro: Náměstí Republiky (B)

GIFTS

Among the best places to go gift shopping are the department stores. Bohemian glass is one of the most popular souvenir choices, and with good reason. You can find some finely crafted pieces at reasonable prices. Onion pattern porcelain from Perlová is also sought after, as i crystal.

GLASS

Czech (actually Bohemian) glass is among the best in the world. Moser – once supplier to the royal court – has some very beautiful pieces. Salon Philadelphia custom engraves all kinds of crystal or glass, from the heaviest vase to the most delicate. Bohemian 'Pirkenhammer' porcelain, from Dubí, is very popular.

Art (F3)
Na Perštýne 10;
Metro: Národní třída (B)

Crystalex (F3)
Malé náměstí 6;
Metro: Staroměstská (A)

Karlovarský porcelán (F3)
Pařižská 2;
Metro: Staroměstská (A)

Moser (F3)
★ *Na příkopě 12;*
Metro: Můstek (A and B)

Salon Philadelphia (F4)
Vodičkova 30;
Metro: Můstek (A and B)

Český porcelán (F3)
Onion shapes from Dubí.
Perlová 10; Metro: Národní třída (B)

JEWELLERY

Prague was long the capital fo deep-red Bohemian granite, a well as jewels from Jablone (where glass and crystal wer once manufactured).

Prague is still a city for art and artists

Böhmische Granate (F3)
Celetná 4;
Metro: Náměstí Republiky (B)

Granát (F2)
★ *Dlouhá třída 28;*
Metro: Náměstí Republiky (B)

Granát (F4)
Vodičkova 31;
Metro: Můstek (A and B)

Holiday (F4)
Národní třída 38;
Metro: Národní třída (B)

JEWELLERY (ANTIQUE)

Interesting pieces may be found at Royal, Na příkopě 12, and in EL' Sure, Václavské náměstí 4.

LACE

The Belgian Queen Fabiola presided over the exhibition of the modern works of Vlasta Wasserbauerová at the 4th International Biennial of Lace, which was held in 1989.

Galerie Vlasta (F3)
★ *Staroměstské náměstí 5;*
Metro: Staroměstská (A)

MUSICAL INSTRUMENTS

Home to such great composers as Mozart, Dvořák and Smetana, Bohemia is steeped in musical tradition and has long been renowned for the manufacture of excellent musical instruments.

Dům hudebních nástrojů (F3)
Jungmannovo náměstí 17;
Metro: Můstek (A and B)

Hudební nástroje (D5,F4)
Štefánikova 19; Metro: Anděl (B)
and *Václavské náměstí 13; Metro:*
Můstek (A and B)

RECORDS & CDs

Good and cheap vinyl records and CDs.

Miláček (G4)
Václavské náměstí 51;
Metro: Muzeum (A and C)

Popron (F4)
★ *Jungmannova 30;*
Metro: Můstek (A and B)

Supraphon (F4)
Jungmannova 20;
Metro: Můstek (A and B)

A good night's sleep

*Luxury hotels and converted palaces, bed and breakfast or a
room in a private house - there is something to suit every
pocket, but be sure to book in advance*

Though there is no shortage of good hotels in Prague, you would be well advised to book a room beforehand. To accommodate the steady flow of tourists a number of new, luxury hotels have recently been built, while some of the traditional establishments have been completely modernized and many of the larger hotels have increased their capacity. Several of the grand old residences, once homes to the nobility, have been renovated and converted into small, luxury hotels. With just a dozen or so rooms, the atmosphere is intimate and they offer the comfort and charm of a bygone age. Bed and breakfast hotels are another recent development. Although generally located outside the town centre, they offer tourists a high standard of accommodation at very reasonable prices. Bear in mind, however, that toilets and bathrooms are shared, usually one per two double rooms. An even cheaper

The Grand Hotel Evropa, opened in 1900, is a monument to the glory of Art Nouveau

option are the small guest houses on the edge of town and the privately owned houses which rent rooms that have generally been refurbished. Two good travel agents specializing in arranging private accommodations are *AVE* and *Pragtour*. *AVE* has branches at the Holešovice station *(07.00-23.00 hrs),* Ruzyně airport *(07.00-22.00 hrs)*, and the Rudná motorway service station 6 km from Prague *(all offices can be contacted on Tel: 24 61 71 33, Fax: 54 97 43); Pragtour* (**F3**), *Old Town Hall; Tel: 24 48 25 62, Fax: 24 28 23 80*. You can also phone, fax or write to the hotel directly *(international dial code 00422)* prior to departure.

For travellers on a tight budget, there are a number of cheap student hostels and these do not just cater for young people. Availability is generally good, especially during the holidays. Although they are located on the outskirts, Prague's highly efficient transport systems make travelling to the heart of the city easy.

Hotels are divided into the normal categories: 5-star luxury, 5-star, 4-star, and so forth. The top hotels, such as the Hotel Inter-Continental and the Diplomat, offer everything you would expect: 24-hour room service, colour TVs and hotel teletext, business centres and conference rooms etc. The largest four-star hotel, the Prague Hilton Atrium, has 1568 rooms. Room prices are in line with those charged by equivalent hotels in other major European cities, but they are slightly lower out of season.

The people of Prague like to eat well – and copiously! Breakfast in hotels or private rooms tends to be quite ample, while some of the hotels lay out a Scandinavian-style breakfast buffet. The food in a good number of the hotel restaurants is first-class, with menus offering fine Bohemian and international dishes. But, although many hotels offer half-board, you may prefer to try out the small, atmospheric eateries dotted around the Little Quarter and Staré Město.

GROUP A HOTELS

Luxury hotels from £90 per night

Ambassador (F3)
★ An Art Nouveau building in the pedestrian precinct of Wenceslas Square. Most rooms are decorated in Louis XV style. The French restaurant serves international cuisine; game is a main feature on the Halali grill menu. Night show. 118 rooms.
Václavské náměstí 5; Tel: 24 19 38 76, 24 21 21 85, Fax: 24 23 06 20; Metro: Můstek (A and B)

Esplanade (G4)
★ Exclusive hotel in a quiet location close to Wenceslas Square.

French restaurant with international cuisine, 'East Wine Restaurant', and live music. 64 rooms.
Washingtonova 19; Tel: 24 21 17 15, Fax: 24 22 93 06; Metro: Muzeum (A and C)

International (O, direction C1)
Built in the wedding-cake style of the 1950s, this hotel is some distance outside the city. Good Bohemian and international cuisine as well as a wine bar with Romany music. 240 rooms.
Dejvice, Koulova 15; Tel: 24 39 31 11, Fax: 24 31 06 16; Metro: Dejvická (A)

Olympik (O, direction I1)
★ This 22-storey hotel in the Karlín quarter has a swimming pool. The Havana club is on the top floor. Parking. 318 rooms; a further 267 rooms in the Dependance Hotel (bed and breakfast).
Karlín Sokolovská 138; Tel: 66 18 11 11, Fax: 66 31 05 59; Metro: Invalidovna (B)

Panorama (O)
A 24-storey hotel not far from the Prague-Brno motorway, opposite the Hotel Forum in Pankrác. Good for long-distance travellers; has a sauna, pool and solarium. 451 rooms and 2 apartments.
Prague 4, Milevská 7; Tel: 61 16 11 11, Fax: 42 10 92; Metro: Pankrác (C)

Parkhotel (G1)
★ Elegant hotel by the Stromovka car park in Letná. Modern restaurant with Bohemian cuisine, Bar-Grill and wine bar with good food. Casino open from 20.00 to 05.00 hrs. Parking. 324 rooms.
Veletržní 20; Tel: 38 07 11 11, Fax: 24 31 61 80; Metro: Vltavská (C)

MARCO POLO SELECTION: HOTELS

1 Ambassador
Impressive hotel in Wenceslas Square (page 72)

2 Prague Hilton Atrium
The biggest hotel in Prague, 786 rooms, two tennis courts (page 74)

3 Esplanade
Nice location opposite a park (page 72)

4 Evropa
Classic example of Art Nouveau splendour (page 75)

5 U Blaženky
Intimate hotel in a tranquil residential area (page 76)

6 Kampa
Quiet hotel on Kampa Island with modern amenities (page 75)

7 Olympik
Well-equipped, 22-storey hotel on the outskirts of town (page 72)

8 Parkhotel
Elegant, modern, with casino (page 72)

9 Renaissance
Newly opened and central (page 73)

10 Vaníček Hotel
Hotel in quiet location with panoramic terraces (page 73)

Paříž (F3)
Built in 1907, this hotel boasts very large rooms. The restaurant, with its Italian mosaic decoration, serves Bohemian and international cuisine in a pleasant *fin-de-siècle* atmosphere. Also has a lovely Art Nouveau café. 100 rooms.
U obecního domu 1, Tel: 24 22 21 51, Fax: 24 22 54 75; Metro: Náměstí Republiky (B)

Renaissance (G3)
★ A new and well-appointed hotel, not far from the Powder Tower. 309 rooms.
V celnici 7; Tel: 24 81 03 96, Fax: 23 81 16 87; Metro: Náměstí Republiky (B)

Tennis-Club-Hotel-Praha (O)
Built in 1991 by a team of Czech and Austrian architects, this sports club features 6 indoor and 4 outdoor tennis courts that may be rented by the hour (the renowned Czech tennis school trains here, too). Offers 96 rooms and 4 apartments, a fitness centre, sauna, swimming pool, squash. Five kilometres from the centre of Prague near the Prague-Brno motorway.
Průhonice 400; Tel: 6 43 65 01

Vaníček Hotel (T) (C4)
★ ☆ Guests at this family-run luxury establishment enjoy an unrivalled panorama of Prague. Includes a good, reasonably priced restaurant with excellent service. Lovely terraces with barbecue. Double room £70 in winter, £95 in season. Shuttle buses serve central Prague. There is a 7% reduction when you pay in cash.
Na Hřebenkách 60; Tel: 35 07 14, Fax: 35 06 19; Metro: Karlovo náměstí (B) and bus 176

Prague Luxury hotels

Adria (F4)

This 4-star hotel right in the centre of the city has been totally renovated. Good international and Bohemian cooking in the Restaurant Triton. 67 rooms, one with disabled access. A double room is £100-125.
Wenceslas Square 26; Tel: 24 21 65 43, Fax: 24 21 10 25; Metro: Můstek (A)

Prague Hilton Atrium (H2)

★ Extremely modern hotel built by a French company in the centre of the city. Largest hotel in Prague with business service centre, conference rooms and restaurants. 788 rooms. Double £125.
Pobřežní ulice; Tel: 24 84 11 11, Fax: 24 81 18 96; Metro: Florenc (B and C)

Diplomat (C1)

Towards the airport. An exclusive, technically refined hotel. Conference rooms for 8 to 350 people. Underground car park. 387 rooms, Double £205.
Dejvice, Evropská třída 15, Tel: 24 39 41 11, Fax: 24 39 42 15; Metro: Dejvická (A)

Forum (O)

Near the motorway to Brno. Bowling, squash, 531 rooms. Double £110.
Nusle, Kongresová; Tel: 61 19 12 18, Fax: 42 06 84; Metro: Vyšehrad (C)

Hoffmeister (E2)

New luxury hotel, very comfortable. Fully air-conditioned. Underground car park, Ada restaurant and Lily wine bar. Excellent food. 44 rooms, from £160.
Pod Bruskou 9; Tel: 24 51 10 15, Fax: 53 09 59; Metro: Malostranská (A)

Intercontinental (F2)

Located in a tranquil spot on the banks of the Vlatva. Panoramic view of the city from the upper floors. Underground car park, 364 rooms, from £135.
Nám. Curieových 5; Tel: 24 88 11 11, Fax: 24 81 12 16; Metro: Staroměstká (A)

Palace (F-G3)

This beautiful Art Nouveau building (1906), fully renovated in 1989, stands opposite the main post office, a stone's throw from Wenceslas Square. Casino, sauna, solarium, underground car park, 125 rooms from £230.
Panská 12; Tel: 24 09 31 11, Fax: 24 22 12 40, Metro: Můstek (A)

Praha (O)

A luxury hotel once favoured by the Party élite. Towards the airport. 124 rooms, £160.
Dejvice, Sušická 20; Tel: 24 34 11 11, Fax: 24 31 12 18; Metro: Dejvická (A)

Savoy (C3)

An excellent (5-star) Art Nouveau hotel not far from the Castle, completely modernized. 58 rooms from £135.
Keplerova 6; Tel: 24 30 21 11, Fax: 24 30 21 28; Metro: Hradčanská (A)

GROUP B HOTELS

Medium priced hotels from around £45 per night

Admirál Botel (E5)
Four boats moored on the banks of the Vltava, converted into a hotel. The Admirál is not far from the road to Plzeň (Plzeňská). 88 twin-bedded cabins with showers and WC. A double is £45-60.
Hořejší nábřeží; Tel: 24 51 16 97; Metro: Anděl (B)

Albatros Botel (F2)
☆ This ship-hotel is anchored not far from the centre, with a lovely view of Hradčany. Discotheque on Friday and Saturday nights. 86 rooms. Double £45-55.
Nábřeží Ludvíka Svobody; Tel: 24 81 12 14; Metro: Náměstí Republiky (B) then an 800-m walk

Belvedere (G1)
A nice hotel in a pleasant area of Prague (Letná). Restaurant, snack bar, and brass band on Thursdays. 117 rooms. Double £42-90.
Milady Horákové 19; Tel: 37 47 41; Metro: Vltavská (B)

Evropa (F4)
★ A classic example of Prague Art Nouveau with many fine details inside, both in the café and in the Pilsner restaurant. 87 rooms. Double around £75.
Václavské náměstí 29; Tel. and Fax: 24 22 81 17; Metro: Muzeum (A)

Golf (O, direction A5)
Hotel with a golf course, 2 km from the end of the Plzeň-Prague motorway. 174 rooms. Double £52-60.
Plzeňská 215a; Tel: 52 32 51, Fax: 52 21 53; Metro: Anděl (B)

Kampa (E3)
★ A completely renovated house known as 'The Old Armoury', located in a tranquil spot on Kampa Island in Mála Strana (Little Quarter). 84 rooms. Double £65-80.
Všehrdova 16; Tel: 24 51 04 09; Metro: Národní třída (B) and tram 9

Karl Inn (I2)
A new 3-star hotel not far from the centre. 168 rooms. Double £45-65.
Saldova 54; Tel: 24 81 17 18, Fax: 24 81 26 81; Metro: Křižíkova (B)

Kern Pension (B6)
A quiet, family-oriented atmosphere prevails in this establishment. Parking in the courtyard. Located in an exclusive residential area to the west of the city, about 4 km from the end of the Plzeň motorway. 14 rooms. Double £35-45.
Jinonická 50; Tel: and Fax: 52 74 80; Metro: Anděl, tram 4, 9 and bus 130.

Pyramida (B3)
This unusual pyramid-shaped hotel is conveniently located near the castle. 350 rooms. Double £60-80.
Břevnov, Bělohorská 24; Tel: 3 11 32 41, Fax: 35 00 30; Metro: Hradčanská (A) and tram 8.

Racek Botel (O)
Prague's third ship-hotel is anchored in the southern part of the city, between Vyšehrad and Braník. Entirely renovated in 1990, it offers the same standards of comfort as the Admirál. Bar with music. Double £45-60.
Na Dvoreckého louce; Tel: 61 21 41 09, Fax: 61 21 43 83; Metro: Karlovo náměstí (B)

Hotel Forum: an ultra-modern high-class hotel on the outskirts of town

U Blaženky (C6)

★ Small, comfortable hotel in a quiet residential area about 5 km from the end of the Plzeň motorway. Offers 9 double rooms and 4 apartments. Double £60-70.
U Blaženky 1; Tel/Fax: 24 51 10 29; Metro: Anděl(B) & bus 137, 3rd stop.

GROUP C HOTELS

Basic hotels from £25 per night

Coubertin (B4)

Modern hotel, in a tranquil part of Strahov. 25 rooms. Double £40-60.
Atletická 4; Tel: 35 28 51; Metro: Karlovo náměstí (B) and bus 176

Junior (F4)

Located on a lively street in the city centre. Good value for the money. All rooms feature shower and WC. Restaurant. 22 rooms. Double 1900 Kč.
Žitná 12; Tel: 29 29 84, Fax: 24 22 39 11; Metro: Muzeum (A) or Karlovo náměstí (B)

The Flemish Spy

The next time you reach for your wallet in Prague, take a few minutes to have a closer look at the Czech banknotes, which were designed by Karel Kulhánek. During the Communist regime, the artist was arrested and charged with trying to make the country appear ridiculous in the eyes of the outside world – an accusation for which Kulhánek was incarcerated. His wife wrote to him in prison, informing him that the police had confiscated his passport, and therefore he would no longer be able to go and visit his old friend Hieronymous Bosch. When a representative from the Czech secret police intercepted the letter, he was incensed and roared at Kulhánek: 'Who does this Bosch work for? What secret information have you passed along to him?' While attempting to keep a straight face, Kulhánek respectfully replied that the artist had been dead for 500 years. In reply to this, the policeman grumbled, 'Bloody intellectuals'.

Kolej J. A. Komenského (B3)

A former student residence, converted into a bed and breakfast hotel. Not far from the Castle. 150 rooms. Double, around £20.
Parléřova 6; Tel: 35 20 40; Metro: Hradčanská (A)

Kupa (0)

This bed and breakfast hotel is in the south of the city, at the terminus of line C. 560 rooms. Double, around £35.
Between Háje and Chodov, Kupeckého 843; Tel: 7 91 03 21, Fax: 7 91 02 16; Metro: Háje (C) (2 minutes' walk)

Rhea (0)

Located at the eastern end of the city, but convenient since it is near a Metro station. One shower and WC for two double rooms. 100 rooms.
Malešice, V úžlabiné 19; Tel: 77 42 97; Metro: Želivského (A) and buses 144, 155, 188, and 208

Tourist (B6)

Modern hotel in a central area, 300 rooms, some laid out like small apartments, with a common kitchen, bathroom and toilets. Snack bar, brasserie and restaurant. Discotheque three nights a week in the good, reasonably priced restaurant, Na Farkáně (about 100 m from the hotel). Double, around £25 including breakfast.
Peroutkova 531; Tel: 52 96 20 62, Fax: 52 96 22 47; Metro: Anděl (B) and bus 137, 5th stop.

STUDENT ACCOMMODATION

Hostel Estec (C4)

Strahov student hall, open from June to end August. 550 beds. *Vaníčkova 5; Tel: 52 73 44; Metro: Dejvická (A) and bus 217, 143; Metro: Karlovo náměstí (B), bus 176, stop: Strahov Stadión*

Hostel Sokol (D3)

Open from May to September. Reasonably priced, and even less expensive if you remember to bring along your own sleeping bag. Located in the Malá Strana (Little Quarter).
Hellichova 1; Tel: 24 51 06 07; Metro: Národní třída (B) and tram 22, 3rd stop

Kolej Jednota (G4)

Not far from the main station (Praha-hlavní nádraží) in the town centre.
Opletalova 38; Tel: 24 21 17 73; Metro: Hlavní nádraží (C)

Kolej Petrská (G2)

This student hall of residence (*kolej*) is open all year round. Ideally located right in the heart of Prague.
Petrská 3; Tel: 231 52 82; Metro: Náměstí Republiky (B)

Větrník (0, direction A3)

Student hall offering 1000 beds in July and August; 40 beds during the rest of the year.
Na větrníku 12; Tel: 38 05; Metro: Hradčanská (A) and bus 1, 18

Universitas Tour (G4)

This is a good place to go for information about cheap accommodation in student halls of residence. Generally, there will be no problem in finding accommodation, not just for students, but for anyone with sufficiently modest requirements.
Opletalova 38; Tel: 26 04 26; Fax: 24 21 22 90

Prague diary

There is no shortage of top class entertainment,
from classical concerts to tennis tournaments

The people of Prague excel in the art of entertainment. After so many years of cultural repression, the streets of the city are animated once again. The annual festivities begin with the New Year which is rung in on Wenceslas Square ★. The arrival of spring in Prague brings with it a wonderful, colourful atmosphere. Snowdrops and violets are sold on street corners and, at Easter, women from South Moravia – often dressed in traditional costume – come into the city to sell their intricately hand-painted Easter eggs. On 1 May, young people lay bouquets of flowers at the memorial to the writer K. H. Mácha on Petřín. From 12 May to 2 June, Prague resonates with music – the 'Prague Spring' festival traditionally opens with a rousing rendition of Smetana's *My Country* by the Prague Philharmonic, and closes with Beethoven's *Ninth Symphony*. In addition to these festivities, a

great number of concerts are staged in the intervening weeks, and folk groups perform southern Bohemian polkas and stirring Moravian folk songs in Prague's gardens and halls throughout the summer months. Concerts are held daily in the city's grandest venues and music halls, including Bertramka, the 'House at the Stone Bell', the Spanish Hall, the Klementinum, the gardens of the Old Palace, and the surrounding churches. Perhaps the most beautiful of all these concert venues is the salon in the Nostic Palace. Many jazz and rock concerts are also staged here, including some big names, drawing in a young and lively crowd. After the short summer break, cultural life recommences in autumn with opening performances held at Prague's ballet, theatre and three opera houses, and by the creative Laterna Magika company. On 28 October, a major music festival is held to celebrate the anniversary of the birth of the Czech Republic, with everything from wind ensembles to hard rock played by groups that gather in the city's public squares. A party spirit

'If you are Bohemian, you are a musician' - there is much truth in this saying. Prague is a 'musical metropolis' rooted in tradition

prevails across the country on 17 November, the anniversary of the Velvet Revolution. At Christmas time, many churches erect nativity scenes. A beautiful Baroque scene (1764) with figures that are almost life-size, can be seen at St Mary's Church in the Capucin monastery, not far from Loreta.

HOLIDAYS

1 January; Easter Monday; 1 May; 8 May; 5 July *(Introduction of Christianity)*; 6 July *(Death of Jan Hus)*; 28 October *(Foundation of the Czech Republic, 1918)*; 24 to 26 December. On public holidays, museums and galleries remain open, while shops and businesses are closed.

SPECIAL EVENTS

January

2-7 January: *Prague Winter* – an important cultural festival, with special performances in theatres, churches and concert halls.

February

Throughout the month, *numerous balls* and gala events are held in the Diplomat, Forum and Prague Hilton Atrium hotels as well as in the Palác kultury.

March

8-26 March: *Festival of Contemporary Music.*
27 March-2 April: *Big Band Jazz Festival* in Reduta.

April

International Jazz Festival when celebrity jazz musicians from Europe and the USA perform in the Palác kultury.

May

9-12 May: *The World of Books.*
★ 12 May-2 June: *Prague Spring* Music festival featuring foreign orchestras and soloists.
30 May-7 Sept: *Rudolf II and Prague* exhibition. More than 2000 exhibits are gathered from all over the world and displayed in the Castle, Ball house, Belvedere, Valdštejn Riding School, and the royal stables. The Castle Gallery will be reopened and will include works of art from Rudolf's collection.
May to October: *Festival of Jewish Culture,* Jubilee Synagogue.

MARCO POLO SELECTION: EVENTS

1 New Year
Celebrations centred around Wenceslas Square (page 79)

2 Prague Spring 12 May-2 June
The city is filled with the sound of music (page 80)

3 'Dance Prague 97'
Festival of contemporary dance (page 81)

4 Škoda Czech Open in August
World class tennis tournament (page 81)

5 Prague Autumn music festival
The Prague orchestra accompanies international soloists (page 81)

6 Christmas crib
Churches beautifully decorated with nativity scenes (page 81)

Folk dancing and rural tradition are still very much alive

June

★ 15 June-3 July: *Dance Prague 97*. International contemporary dance festival. In the National Theatre, Archa Theatre and Akropolis.

26-30 June: *Agharta* International jazz festival, Krakovská 5.

20-22 June: *International Folklore Festival* in Strážnice.

15 June-7 July: *Prague Music Days* (Bruckner, Romantic music and Mozart).

July

11-13 July: *KB Open* in which the top eight women champion tennis players, such as Martinez and Fernandez, compete.

August

★ 28 July-3 August: *Škoda Czech Open* ATP tennis tournament

22 August: *Young Prague* 14 day international festival of music for musicians between 17-30.

September

7-24 September: *Praha Europa Musica Festival* under the patronage of the Council of Europe and organized by Italy.

★ 12-21 September: *Prague Autumn Festival* in the Dvořák Hall in the Rudolfinum.

8-16 September: Pottery market on Kampa Island under the Charles Bridge.

October

In Pardubice, 100 km east of Prague, the *Great Pardubice Steeplechase* (since 1874), the most difficult horse race in Europe, is held on the second Sunday (30 hurdles and a 6.5 m ditch).

28 October: Anniversary of the foundation day of the Czech Republic in 1918. Celebrated with concerts, and various rooms in Prague Castle that are not normally accessible are opened to the public.

November

17 November: Anniversary of the Velvet Revolution of 1989.

December

★ 24 December- early February: church nativity scenes; the best at St Vitus Cathedral and St Mary's Church on Loretánské náměstí.

Out on the town

*Opera and pantomime, classical concerts and jazz,
cabarets and clubs, traditional bands in old pubs…
entertainment to suit every mood and taste*

Prague specializes in musical and comic entertainment. Even the classical revues, such as those performed at the Alhambra or by the famed Laterna Magika company, usually incorporate some humorous element. The musical tradition is continued not only in the concert halls, but also on the streets and in bars, where jazz and brass bands are always popular. The old Czech cabaret U Fleků is well worth a visit.

BOAT TRIPS

A boat trip along the Vltava is an unforgettable experience. A variety of boats cater for all tastes – for a touch of old world charm, try one of the paddle-steamers. Dinner cruises with musical accompaniment make for a romantic night out. The Prague Panorama excursions are recommended (both long and short trips are offered). Bookings: (**F2**) *Čedok Travel Agents; Pařížská 6; Tel: 231 82 55; Metro: Staroměstská (A)*

Prague National Theatre where great classics are staged: the Operas of Smetana are regularly performed here

and (**E5**) *Paroplavba, Rašínovo nábřeží (next to the Palackého Bridge). Tel: 29 38 03 and 24 91 38 62; Metro: Karlovo náměstí (B), 200 m from the river*

CABARETS & REVUES

These elegant establishments stage some excellent late-night shows. A variety of genres are often mixed: music, dance, ballet, mime, comedy sketches, etc. The unique Black Theatre is particularly popular – actors dressed in black move objects in front of a black background, so that they appear to have a life of their own.

Alhambra Revue (F3)
★ 90-minute variety show (Alhambra Revue and Bohemian Fantasy) featuring ballet, music, cabaret and 'black theatre'.
Daily (except Sun) 19.00-02.00 hrs; Václavské náměstí 5-7; Metro: Můstek (A and B)

Hotel International (O, direction C1)
★ Wine parties are held in the garden pavilion. Entertainment in the form of lively traditional songs accompanied

by brass and percussion.
Daily 19.30 hrs; Dejvice, Koulova 15; Tel: 24 39 31 11; Metro: Dejvická (A)

U Fleků (E4)
★ ۞ The epitome of old Czech cabaret: strong beer to drink and old standards sung with great feeling.
Tues-Sat from 19.30 hrs; Křemencova 11; Tel: 24 91 51 18; Metro: Národní třída (B)

Variété Praga (F4)
International programme of artists and dancers.
Vodičkova 30; Tel: 24 21 59 45, 24 21 12 46; Metro: Můstek (A and B)

CASINOS

Admirál (F4)
Try your hand at roulette, poker, baccarat or black jack.
Daily 13.00-05.00 hrs; Vodičkova 30; Metro: Můstek (A and B)

Casino de France (H2)
Roulette, black jack, chemin de fer, punto banco. Prague Hilton Atrium Hotel.
Daily 14.00-06.00 hrs; Pobřežní 1; Metro: Florenc (B and C)

Casino Palais Savarin (F3)
Roulette, black jack, poker.
Daily 13.00-04.00 hrs; Na příkopě 10; Metro: Můstek (A and B)

Forum Hotel (0)
Three roulette tables, two for black jack.
Daily 20.00-04.00 hrs; Nusle, Kongresová 1; Tel: 61 19 11 71; Metro: Vyšehrad (C)

Parkhotel (F1)
Classic casino with roulette and black jack.

Daily 20.00-05.00 hrs; Veletržní 20; Metro: Vltavská (C)

CONCERTS

Prague is a wonderful place for classical music lovers. The Czech Philharmonic, the Prague Symphony Orchestra FOK and the Prague Radio Symphony Orchestra perform all year round. Performances of the Prague Madrigals, Musica Bohemica, Czech Nonettes and the Smetana Quartet are held in such splendid venues as the Mirrored Chapel of the Klementinum, the 'House at the Stone Bell', the Prague Salon in the Nostic Palace, the Spanish Hall and the Mozart Museum at Bertramka. During the summer season, concerts are also held in the beautifully landscaped Prague Palace Gardens. Glorious church music can be heard in St Vitus Cathedral, and in the churches of St Nicholas and St Jakob. Programme guides are produced monthly.

DISCOS

There are plenty of discos in Prague, some of which are quite surreal, and they are not just confined to the centre. Since the Velvet Revolution, dance trends have veered towards rap and rock, but you can find music to suit all tastes. Bear in mind that Prague nightlife starts early and many of the discos are jam-packed by 20.30!

Disco-Club (0)
In the Hotel Panorama in Pankrác, on the first floor. A good all-around disco.
Daily 21.00-03.00 hrs; Milevská 7; Tel: 61 16 11 11; Metro: Pankrác (C)

MARCO POLO SELECTION: NIGHT-TIME ENTERTAINMENT

1 Alhambra Revue
Songs and ballet on Wenceslas Square (page 83)

2 Zlatá husa Video-Disko
Best disco in town (page 85)

3 Laterna magika
World renowned theatre (page 88)

4 Národní divadlo – National Theatre
Opera and ballet in the 'Golden chapel' (page 87)

5 Belmondo Revival Club
Top rock venue (page 88)

6 Křižík fountains
Choreographed aquatic show (page 88)

7 Puppet theatre
Don Giovanni in miniature (page 88)

8 Wine party
Traditional song and dance, and plenty of wine *al fresco* (page 83)

9 Reduta Jazz
Longest-running jazz club in town (page 85)

10 U Fleků
Brass bands and beer beneath the trees (page 84)

Lávka Club (E3)

♣ Excellent place, and not just for the young crowd. Located next to the Smetana Museum; there is also dancing on the terrace in the garden.
Daily 21.00-05.00 hrs; Novotného lávka 1; Metro: Staroměstská (A)

Musicpark (H5)

There's little chance of getting bored here. It's the biggest disco in the city, which also features a café, restaurant, bar and casino.
Daily (except Mon) 21.00-05.00 hrs; Francouzská 4; Tel: 691 14 91; Metro: Náměstí miru (A)

Video-Disko Zlatá husa (F3)

★ The best disco in Prague. Occasionally invites foreign guest DJs.
Daily 20.30-01.30 hrs; Václavské náměstí 5-7; Tel: 24 19 31 11; Metro: Můstek (A and B)

JAZZ

Many international musicians played in Prague before the war, when the foxtrot was all the rage. Today, jazz continues to be very popular in the city and some of the world's major musicians come to perform here, although the country has its own great talents such as the flute virtuoso Jiří Stivín, pianist Emil Viklický, Lípa, Šeban and his quartet, the 'Original Synkopický Orchestra' directed by O. Havelka, or the Petr Binder Blues Band. The best jazz club is the ★ 'Reduta' – founded in 1958, it is the oldest running jazz venue in Europe. While on an official visit to Prague in January 1994, Bill Clinton took a break from matters of state, unpacked his saxophone and played 'Summertime' and

'My Funny Valentine' here. Václav Havel accompanied him, and the charm of the impromptu performance compensated for any technical shortcomings.

(F4) *Reduta, Národní třída 20;*
(G4) *Agharta Jazz Centre, Krakovská 5 (with Jazz shop and café);*
(F4) *Metropolitan Jazz Club, Jungmannova 14;* **(E4)** *Viola, Národní třída 7*

MUSICALS

A new fashion for musicals has developed in Prague and good performances can be seen at *Výstaviště* **(O** towards **G1)**, *Metro: Holešovické nádraží (C)* and at the *Palace of Culture* **(O** towards **F6)**, *Metro: Vyšehrad (C).* Top hits of the moment include Andrew Lloyd Webber's early classic 'Jesus Christ Superstar' and 'Dracula'.

NIGHTCLUBS

Less noisy and more sophisticated than the new discotheques, these venues have no set musical programme, but the atmosphere is generally friendly and intimate.

Est Bar   (F4)
Music and dancing.
Daily (except Sun) 19.00-02.00 hrs; Hotel Esplanade, Washingtonova 19; Tel: 24 21 17 15; Metro: Muzeum (A and C)

Galaxie Nightclub   (O)
An intimate bar with music and dancing that stays open until the small hours.
Hotel Forum, Kongresová 1; Tel: 61 19 11 75; Metro: Vyšehrad (C)

Noční klub   (H2)
Prague's newest nightclub is as elegant as the rest of the Hotel Atrium where it is located. Very good sound system.
Pobřežní 3; Tel: 24 84 11 11; Metro: Florenc (B and C)

Skyline   (C1)
Good music in the luxury Hotel Diplomat.
Dejvice, Evropská 15; Tel: 24 39 41 11; Metro: Dejvická (A)

OPERA & BALLET

On the Smetana quay stands the beautiful Neo-renaissance Národní divadlo (National Theatre), fondly known as the 'golden chapel by the Vltava' among the people of Prague. The classic show here is Smetana's opera *Libuše.* Not far from the National Museum is the Prague State Opera (*Státní opera Praha*), the former Neue Deutsche Theater, with its lovely Neorococo interior. Mozart's *Don Giovanni* premiered at the Stavovské divadlo (now the shiny

---

Pigeons

The bane of the city, Prague's pigeons have grown up in such a cultured environment and have developed such exquisite tastes that they seek out the city's finest statues, palaces and buildings for leaving unpleasant mementos. Unfortunately, all efforts to rid the city of such 'decor' have failed – everything from pills to poison and more sinister methods have been tried, all in vain. Do not feed them – you will be fined for it.

Prague has a strong cinematic culture

green and gold Estates Theatre), near the centre of the city, in 1787. All three theatres stage world class opera and ballet performances, except during the summer months.

Národní divadlo – National Theatre (E4)
★ For Smetana fans.
Národní třída (B)

Státní opera Praha – Prague State Opera (G4)
Original-language performances.
Wilsonova 4; Tel: 24 22 76 93 and 24 22 98 98; Metro: Muzeum (A and C)

Stavovské divadlo – Estates Theatre (F3)
The theatre provides simultaneous English translation.
Ovocný trh 1; Tel: 24 21 43 39, 24 22 85 03; Metro: Můstek (A and B)

For lovers of opera and operetta, the following performances, regularly given by the Prague Music Theatre, are recommended:
A night with Mozart at the Mozart Museum, Bertramka (**C5**)
Enchanting Dvořák at the Dvořák museum (**F5**)
The Prague Operetta Gala Evening in the Kaiserštejnský Palais (**D3**) (presented in English and German).

PANTOMIME & PUPPET THEATRE

Almost every visitor to Prague will want to see the celebrated Laterna Magika show, first performed in Brussels in 1958 to great (and enduring) acclaim. Other attractions include the puppet theatre which has given over 800 performances of *Don Giovanni*, the Black Theatre and the avant-garde shows of the Ta Fantastika Theatre starring the singer, Lucie Bílá.

Laterna Magica (F4)
★ Original stage performances, an elaborate multimedia experience. Nová scéna.
Národní 4 (next to the National Theatre); Tel: 24 91 41 29, Fax: 24 22 75 67; Metro: Národní třída (B)

Puppet theatre (E3)
★ Mozart's *Don Giovanni* is a perennial hit.
Žatecká 1; Metro: Náměstí republiky (B)

Ta Fantastika (E3)
Karlova 8; Tel: 24 22 90 78; Metro: Staroměstská (A)

ROCK

There are some good rock clubs in Prague. A few years ago the French newspaper *Le Figaro* wrote a travel piece on Prague,

saying that a trip to Prague was worthwhile just for the Castle and the Belmondo Club. Recommended:

★ *Belmondo Revival Club* (**H1**), *Bubenská 1; Metro: Vltavská (C)*
Bunkr (**G2**), *Lodecká 2; Metro: Náměstí republiky (B)*
Rock Café (**E4**), *Národní třída 20; Metro: Národní třída (B)*
Legenda (**E3**), *Křižovnická 12; Metro: Staroměstská (A)*

SON ET LUMIERE

The ★ Křižík fountain in Výstaviště provides an unforgettable spectacle of music, water and light. (**O** towards **G1**)
Výstaviště ; Metro: Holešovické nádraží (C), tram: 5, 12, 17

WINEBARS WITH ROMANY MUSIC

Halali-Restaurant (F3)
Violin music while you dine at the Hotel Ambassador, which serves seasonal game and Hungarian specialities.
Václavské náměstí 5-7, Metro: Můstek (A and B)

Šumická vinárna (C4)
✿ In the deep cellar rooms, good food and drink, and a Romany band with dancing.
Mikulandská 12; Metro: Národní třída (B)

Practical information

*Important addresses and other useful information
for your visit to Prague*

AIRLINE INFORMATION

Čedok
For airline and train reservations.
*49 Southwark Street, London SE1;
Tel: 0171 378 6009, Fax: 0171 403
2321*

Czech Airlines
*72 Margaret Street, London, W1;
Tel: 0171 255 1898*

BANKS & MONEY

The Czech unit of currency is the crown (*koruna - Kč*) which is divided into 100 heller (*halér*). Bank notes come in denominations of 20, 50, 100, 200, 500, 1000, 2000 and 5000 Kč. Most hotels, shops and restaurants will be happy to accept payment by credit card.

The normal opening hours for banks are from 09.00-12.00 hrs and 13.00-16.00 hrs. The majority of banks and bureaux de change are concentrated on and around Wenceslas Square and Na příkopě. It's worth noting that banks charge a commission of 1-2%, while bureaux de change commission charges can be anything between 4 and 9%.

CUSTOMS

Souvenirs and gifts can be exported duty-free. Objets d'art and antiques, however, can only be exported with the official permission of the Czech authorities. Further information can be obtained from the *Customs Office* (**F4**); *Wenceslas Square 24; Tel: 24 22 61 17.* Every customs office provides a list of all the items for which exportation is prohibited; needless to say, these regulations should be followed to the letter.

One regulation that has recently been introduced stipulates that all visitors to the Czech Republic should carry at least 500 Kč per day in cash or its equivalent in foreign currency. This law is being implemented in an attempt to reduce the numbers of illegal workers.

DRIVING

The speed limits are: 60 km/h in urban areas; elsewhere 90 km/h, and 110 km/h on the motorway. *Breakdown service: ABA; Tel: 124 and 123; Autoklub České republiky; Information centre; Opletalova 29; Tel: 24 22 18 20* (**G4**)

Cubism in Prague

Czech Cubism, reflected in both the architecture and furniture, developed between 1911-24. There are many fine examples of the art form in Prague: the semi-detached house at Tychonova 268 (Gočár), Celetná 34 (Gočár), Neklanova 3 (Chochol) and in Vyšehrad, just in front of the railway tunnel (Rašínovo nábřeží), houses 6, 8, 10 and 12. There is also a unique collection of Cubist furniture exhibited at the Arts and Craft Museum (Janák, Chochol, Hofman).

EMBASSIES

Britain **(D2)**
Thunovská 14, Malá Strana
Tel: 24 51 05 32
Metro: Malostranská (A)

Canada **(D3)**
Mickwiczova 6, Prague 6
Tel: 24 31 11 08
Metro: Hradčanská

USA **(D3)**
Trižiště 15, Malá Strana
Tel: 24 51 08 47
Metro: Malostranská (A)

EMERGENCIES

Ambulance: Tel: 155
Breakdown: Tel: 124
Police: Tel: 158 (free)
(see also Medical Assistance)

FOREIGN LANGUAGE GUIDES

If you want a more in depth understanding of the country's historical background and cultural riches, it is a good idea to hire a foreign language guide, particularly when visiting the Royal Castle and the Jewish Museum.

Guides to Prague Castle **(D2)**
Second courtyard (Chapel of the Holy Cross); Tel: 33 37/33 68

Guides to the Jewish Museum (E2)
Klausen synagogue, Maiselova; Tel: 231 03 02 and 231 71 91

GEOGRAPHY

Area: 497 sq km. Inhabitants: 1.3 million (1994). Latitude: 50° North, Longitude: 14° East. Average altitude: 235 m. Climate: average temperature in July 19.2°C; in January 0°C. Vltava: length in Prague 30.9 km; average depth, 3 to 4 metres; greatest width, 330 m. 10 islands, 18 bridges. Number of towers: approx 500.

GUIDED TOURS

Čedok **(F3)**
Mon-Fri 08.30-19.00 hrs, Sat/Sun 09.00-14.00 hrs; Na přikopě 18; Tel: 24 19 71 11; Metro: Můstek (A and B)

Bohemia Ticket International (G4)
Václavské náměstí 25; Tel: 24 22 72 53; Metro: Můstek (A and B)

LISTINGS

Monthly listings are available from the Bohemian Ticket International office.
Václavské náměstí 25 and Na přikopě.

AVE (G3)

Main station, Metro: Hlavní nádraží (C). Holešovice station, airport and at the 'Rudná' service station 6 km outside Prague (towards Plzeň), Tel: 24 61 71 33, Fax: 54 97 43

MEDICAL ASSISTANCE

Nemocnice Na Homolce (O, direction A5)
24 hrs accident and emergency service:
*Roentgenova 2, Prague 5
Tel: 52 92 11 11*

*Doctor: Tel: 52 92 28 31
Surgeon: Tel: 52 92 24 01
Orthopaedic: Tel: 52 92 24 04*

PETROL

The number of service stations on the main routes is increasing all the time. Unleaded petrol is known as Natural (95 octane), Four-star is called Super (96 octane), and a third option is Special (91 octane). Petrol costs from 19-22 Kč. Diesel is called Nafta and costs 16-17 Kč. There are a number of 24 hour petrol stations:

*Smíchov, Plzeňská (**A5**)
Holešovice, Argentinská (**F1**)
Žižkov, Olšanská (**F4**)*

PHARMACY

Lékárna (D5)
Daily 24 hours; Štefánikova 6, Prag 5; Metro: Anděl (B)

POST & TELEPHONE

Post offices (*Pošta*) are easily identified by their large orange sign. The main post office at Jindřišská 14 (**G3**) is open 24 hours a day. Stamps for letters (20g) to all European countries cost 8 Kč and postcards are 5 Kč. Letters to destinations outside Europe will cost 8 Kč and postcards are 6 Kč.

If you want to phone abroad, dial the country code first (0044 for the UK, 00353 for Ireland, and 001 for Canada and the USA), followed by the local number omitting the zero prefix. Local calls cost 2 Kč and telephone cards (valid for national and international calls) are available from post offices and newsagents.

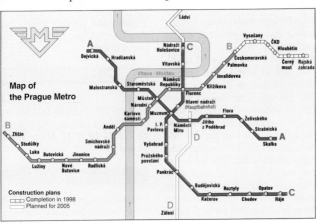

Map of the Prague Metro

Construction plans
Completion in 1998
Planned for 2005

PRAGUE INFORMATION

Čedok (F3)
Mon-Fri 08.30-18.00 hrs, Sat 09.00-14.00 hrs; Na příkopě; Tel: 24 19 71 11; Metro: Můstek (A and B)

Pragotur (F3)
Located in the Old Town Hall in Staroměstské náměstí.
Tel: 24 48 25 62, Fax: 24 28 23 80; Metro: Staroměstská (A)

PRONUNCIATION

Pronunciation of the Czech language is not easy, but the following guidelines should at least help you to read some of the street names and menu items:

The accented vowels á, é, í, ó, ú are all long; the consonant č is pronounced 'ch' as in 'church', while c sounds like ts; h is always pronounced; j sounds like y; ň is like the 'ni' in 'onion'; š sounds like the 'sh' in 'ship'; ř sounds like r and ž combined; ž sounds like the s in pleasure.

PUBLIC TRANSPORT

The Prague underground is the fastest and most efficient way to get around the city. There are three lines: A is green, B is yellow, and C is red. The deepest metro station is Náměstí miru (A) (52 m). One ticket, which can be used for the metro, tram and bus, costs 10 Kč and is valid for one hour during the day, and 90 minutes in the evenings and on weekends. For just 5 Kč you can travel for 15 minutes or 4 stops on the metro. Children under six travel free and under 15 year-olds travel for half-price.

Tickets are available from station machines, newsagents and tobacconists. The metro runs from 05.00 to 24.00 hrs.

The tram system is an efficient alternative, with the added advantage that you can sightsee as you travel.

TAXI

Taxis are plentiful in Prague, and can be hailed anywhere in the street. The basic charge is 30 Kč then 16 Kč per km. A recommended company is Rony Taxi Tel: 43 04 03.

THEATRE TICKETS

PIS (F3)
Mon-Fri 09.00-19.00 hrs, Sat and Sun 09.00-17.00 hrs; Na příkopě 20; Tel: 26 40 23; Metro: Můstek (A and B)

Bohemia Ticket International
Mon-Fri 09.00-13.00 hrs and 14.00-18.00 hrs, Sat 09.00-16.00 hrs, Sun 09.00 - 14.00 hrs; Václavske náměstí 25 (G4) and Na příkopě 16 (F3); Tel: 24 22 72 53

Theatre and concert tickets can also be purchased through the larger hotels.

TICKETS (INTERNAL FLIGHTS)

Čedok (F3)
Mon-Fri 08.30-19.00 hrs, Sat and Sun 09.00-14.00 hrs; Na příkopě 18, Tel: 24 19 71 11; Metro: Můstek (A and B)

TIPPING

It is standard practice to tip waiters in both cafés and restaurants.

as well as taxi drivers, guides, porters, chamber maids and hotel staff. If you wish to make a table reservation, a small tip is recommended.

TOILETS

Toilets are marked WC, 'Dámy' or 'Ženy' for women and 'Páni' or 'Muži' for men.

TOURIST INFORMATION

The Prague Information Service gives tourist and accommodation information, and sells maps and theatre tickets.

PIS (F3)
Mon-Fri 09.00-19.00 hrs, Sat and Sun 09.00-17.00 hrs; Na příkopě 20; Tel: 26 40 23; Metro: Můstek (A/B)

PIS (F3)
Mon-Fri 09.00-19.00 and Sat/Sun 09.00-18.00; Old Town Hall; Tel: 24 48 22 02; Metro: Můstek (A/B)

VISAS

British, Irish, American and most EU nationals require only a valid passport, but Canadian and Australian nationals need to obtain a visa (valid for 30 days).

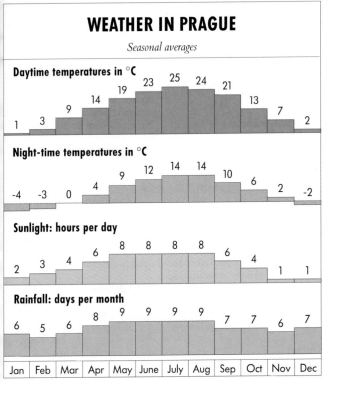

WEATHER IN PRAGUE

Seasonal averages

Daytime temperatures in °C

Jan	Feb	Mar	Apr	May	June	July	Aug	Sep	Oct	Nov	Dec
1	3	9	14	19	23	25	24	21	13	7	2

Night-time temperatures in °C

Jan	Feb	Mar	Apr	May	June	July	Aug	Sep	Oct	Nov	Dec
-4	-3	0	4	9	12	14	14	10	6	2	-2

Sunlight: hours per day

Jan	Feb	Mar	Apr	May	June	July	Aug	Sep	Oct	Nov	Dec
2	3	4	6	8	8	8	8	6	4	1	1

Rainfall: days per month

Jan	Feb	Mar	Apr	May	June	July	Aug	Sep	Oct	Nov	Dec
6	5	6	8	9	9	9	9	7	7	6	7

Do's and don'ts!

Some tips on how to avoid the traps and pitfalls
the unwary traveller may fall into

Driving offences

Given the absolute ban on drinking and driving, avoid all alcoholic beverages (even beer) if you plan to get behind the wheel. What's more, the fine has been increased to 15 'Palackýs' (a 1000 Kč note named after the historian František Palackš, whose picture appears on it). Speeding will cost you two 'Palackýs'.

Money

The 'redistribution of private wealth' is a common practice in Prague! Pickpockets make good business here, so keep your purse or wallet safe, especially in the more crowded tourist areas.

Money changers

You should change money either at the border, or in hotels, bureaux de change or banks. Banks charge a 1-2% commission fee while the private bureaux de change charge 4-9%. Avoid the money changers on the streets as they often distribute counterfeit notes.

Parking

There are several public car parks in the city centre. The main ones are under the National Theatre, at the Rudolfinum and next to the State Opera. If you park illegally, your car will most certainly be towed away. Either that, or you will be clamped and forced to pay a heavy fine.

Taxi drivers

Make sure that your taxi driver has his meter switched on. The licence number should always be written on a standard receipt. No claims can be made if it has not been included. If in doubt you can always try to negotiate the fare in advance!

Thieves' favourite cars

There are a number of international car thief gangs whose favourite targets are Volkswagen Golfs and Audis. Always make sure your car is secure or it will quickly disappear to the East.

White clothing

The move to oil-burning power stations is progressing slowly but coal is still used for fuel, which does pollute the atmosphere. It might be wise to avoid wearing white clothes when walking around Prague.

INDEX

This index lists all the main sights, museums, restaurants and hotels mentioned in this guide.

Sights

Belvedere 14
Bethlehem chapel 22
Charles Bridge 4, 12, 20
Charles University 15
Churches 22
Clementinum 15
Coronation Procession 16
Districts 34
Fred and Ginger 19
House at the Black Madonna 41
House at the Stone Bell 19
Hradčany 4, 30, 31
Kampa 27
Křižovnické náměstí 28
Loreta 16
New Jewish Cemetery 20
Obecní dům 17
Old Jewish Cemetery 21
Old Town Hall 15, 18
Palaces 25
Parks and Gardens 27
Powder Tower 17, 18
Royal Garden 28
Staré Město bridge tower 12, 18
Staroměstské náměstí 29
Theatres 36
Vyšehrad 21
Wenceslas Square (Václavské náměstí) 8, 30

Museums

Art and Crafts museum 46
Bilek gallery 41
Convent of sv Anežka 40
Dvořák museum 41
Jewish Museum 46
Kafka museum 42
Modern Art Exhibition 41
Mozart museum Bertramka 40
Museum of Prague 43
Museum of Military History 46
National gallery 43
National museum 38, 42, 44
Old Bohemian Art 45
Postage museum 44
Rudolfinum 17
Smetana museum 44
Strahov monastery 45, 47
Technical Museum 43

Restaurants

Čertovka 55
Česká hospodá 60
Club Restaurant 56
David 57
Evropa 60
Flambée 56
Gany's 58
Gourmet 56
Halali-Restaurant 57
John Bull 57
Jo's bar 61
Kampa club 57
Klášterní vinárna 57
Klub novinařů 61
Košer restarace 58
Letenský zámeček 58
Lobkovická vinárna 57
Makarská 61
Malostranská beseda 61
Molly Mallone's 57
Monica 58
Myslivna 58
Nebozízek 57
Opera Grill 56
Pálava 61
Parnas 57
Pelikán 58
Red Hot and Blues 57
Rostov 61
Tři grácie 61
U čerta 61
U Fleků 61
U Golema 59
U kalicha 62
U kamenného stolu 59
U krále brabanstkého 62
U Lorety 59
U malého Glena 62
U mecenáše 56
U pastýřky 59
U pavouka 56
U Pešků 62
U Plebana 59
U Rudolfa 62
U Schnellů 62
U staré synagogy 58
U supa 62
U sv. Jana Nepomuckého 59
U svatého Tomáše 63
U tří housliček 63
U Vladaře 58
U zlaté hrušky 56
U zlaté podkovy 60
U zlaté studné 59
Valdštejnská hosp. 60
Vikárka 60
Znojemská vinárna 60

Hotels

Admirál Botel 75
Adria 74
Albatros Botel 75
Ambassador 72
Atrium 74
Belvedere 75
Coubertin 76
Diplomat 74
Esplanade 72
Evropa 70, 75
Forum 74, 76
Golf 75
Hoffmeister 74
Hostel Estec 77
Hostel Sokol 77
Intercontinental 74
International 72
Junior 76
Kampa 75
Karl Inn 75
Kern 75
Kolej J. A. Komenského 77
Kolej Jednota 77
Kolej Petrská 77
Kolej Větrník 77
Kupa 77
Olympik 72
Palace 74
Panorama 72
Paříž 73
Parkhotel 72
Praha 74
Pyramida 75
Racek Botel 75
Renaissance 73
Rhea 77
Savoy 74
Tennis-Club-Hotel-Praha 73
Tourist 77
U Blaženky 76
Vaníček 73

What do you get for your money?

Despite the recent high inflation, many of the goods and services on offer in Prague are still relatively cheap as compared with Western Europe. The currency of the Czech Republic is the Czech crown – koruna česká. The official exchange rate of the crown (Kč) is now reasonably stable.

In August 1996, one pound sterling was worth roughly 40 Kč and one dollar was worth around 25 Kč. Calculating on the basis of this rate, 100 Kč is worth approximately £2.50 or $4. Conversely £100 is equivalent to around 4000 Kč, and $100 is about 2500 Kč.

Hotel prices are not regulated, and during the summer and peak periods, such as Easter and Whitsun they can rise quite sharply. Private accommodation and rooms in guesthouses provide cheap options to the hotels with prices averaging between 400 and 600 Kč per person per day.

If you wish to venture further out, excursions to some of the beautiful chateaux in the surrounding areas of Prague – the imperial palace at Karlštejn or the ducal palace at Konopiště for example – can be quite cheap. One-day or half-day excursions to the castles of southern Bohemia, or the cosmopolitan town of Karlovy Vary, even boat trips down the Vltava can all be enjoyed for a reasonable price.

Here are a few sample prices to give you an idea of what you can get for your money. A single journey on the metro, on a tram or on a bus costs 10 Kč. A bus tour of the city costs 350- 400 Kč. Tickets for museums cost between 30 and 90 Kč and a theatre ticket costs between 120 and 500 Kč A half litre glass of Pilsner beer will cost 13-70 Kč, a glass of cola 10-20 Kč and 0.33 ml of mineral water 10-15 Kč. The prices of alcoholic drinks vary enormously: 5cl Becherovka costs 20-50 Kč, imported Scotch 60-120 Kč. A vinyl record costs 120-180 Kč, a CD 230-300 Kč, and a foreign language cassette is about 150-500 Kč. A postcard costs 3-5 Kč for which a stamp will cost 5 Kč within Europe and 6 Kč outside Europe (letters cost 8 Kč per 20 g). A local telephone call is 2 Kč.